The Dorling Kindersley

ILLUSTRATED
FAMILY
ENCYCLOPEDIA

VOLUME 3 CONTENTS, BENIN EMPIRE – CAVES

DK

LONDON, NEW YORK, MUNICH, MELBOURNE AND DELHI

Senior Editor Jayne Parsons   **Senior Art Editor** Gillian Shaw

Project Editors
Marian Broderick, Gill Cooling,
Maggie Crowley, Hazel Egerton,
Cynthia O'Neill, Veronica Pennycook,
Louise Pritchard, Steve Setford, Jackie Wilson

Project Art Editors
Jane Felstead, Martyn Foote,
Neville Graham, Jamie Hanson,
Christopher Howson, Jill Plank, Floyd Sayers,
Jane Tetzlaff, Ann Thompson

Editors
Rachel Beaugié, Nic Kynaston, Sarah Levete,
Karen O'Brien, Linda Sonntag

Art Editors
Tina Borg, Diane Clouting,
Tory Gordon-Harris

DTP Designers
Andrew O'Brien, Cordelia Springer

Managing Editor Ann Kramer   **Managing Art Editor** Peter Bailey

Senior DTP Designer Mathew Birch

Picture Research Jo Walton, Kate Duncan, Liz Moore

DK Picture Library Ola Rudowska, Melanie Simmonds

Country pages by PAGE*One*: Bob Gordon, Helen Parker,
Thomas Keenes, Sarah Watson, Chris Clark

Cartographers Peter Winfield, James Anderson

Research Robert Graham, Angela Koo

Editorial Assistants Sarah-Louise Reed, Nichola Roberts

Production Louise Barratt, Charlotte Traill

First published in Great Britain in 1997, 2004
by Dorling Kindersley Limited,
80 Strand, London WC2R 0RL

Copyright © 1997, © 2004 Dorling Kindersley Limited, London
A Penguin company

This edition published in 2004 by MDS BOOKS/MEDIASAT Group in association with MediaFund Limited

www.mediasatgroup.com

A CIP catalogue record for this book is available from the British Library

ISBN: 84 9789 537 1 (ISBN of the collection)
ISBN: 84 9789 522 3 (ISBN of this volume)
ISSN: 1744 2214

Not to be sold separately from the Daily Mail

Colour reproduction by Colourscan, Singapore
Printed and bound in the E.U.

BENIN EMPIRE

ESTABLISHED IN THE 11TH CENTURY, Benin was a powerful West African kingdom which flourished in the forests west of the River Niger. The wealth of Benin was based on trading: trans-Saharan trade with African savannah kingdoms, which linked the Benin Empire with the Mediterranean and the Middle East, and, coastal trade with Europeans. Benin's obas, or kings, controlled the trade networks. Immensely powerful, they lived in the royal palace in the capital city of Benin. In 1897, the British conquered Benin and ended the empire.

Empire boundaries

The Benin Empire was in modern Nigeria, where Benin City now stands. Both it and the modern republic west of Nigeria take their name from the old empire.

Sahara Desert

• Benin City

Benin City

The empire of Benin was centred on the impressive capital, Benin City. A wide road ran through the centre, and a huge earthwork wall surrounded the city. The wall acted as a defence and would have taken some considerable time to build. Its size stood as a symbol of the influence held by Benin's oba. The city housed the oba's royal palace, and areas called wards where the craftspeople lived.

Engraving of Benin City

Craft guilds

Guilds of craftspeople, such as leather workers, blacksmiths, drummers, weavers, carpenters, ivory carvers, and brass casters lived in Benin City. The brass casters formed one of the most important guilds. They made the distinctive "bronze" heads and plaques for the royal palace.

Spikes to support ivory carving

Only obas wore neck rings.

Bronze head
Benin "bronze" heads are actually made of brass. They commemorated dead obas and their family members, court ceremonies – even European traders. Carved ivory adorned the heads, which were kept in shrines in the royal palace.

Memorial head of an oba

Obas and courtiers wore ornamental weapons on ceremonial occasions.

Oba flanked by two courtiers

Carvings often told of the oba's wealth and military strength.

Carved human figures

Carved elephant's tusk

Brass plaques
Carved plaques decorated the wooden pillars that supported the oba's palace roof. They depicted court life and important events, such as the presentation of gifts from the oba to his courtiers.

Ivory carving
Ornately carved ivory tusks were among Benin's luxury goods. All trade in ivory was controlled by the oba. If elephant hunters killed an elephant, they had to give one tusk to the oba before they could sell the other.

Trade

For centuries, Benin traded with African kingdoms to the north, including the Songhai Empire. The arrival of the Europeans in the 1400s disrupted these traditional relationships and established new trading outlets.

Brass manilla

Brass manillas
In Benin, merchants used bracelet-shaped objects called manillas to buy expensive purchases, but they used tiny, white cowrie shells for smaller items.

Merchants
Travelling by sea, Portuguese traders bought slaves, peppers, cloth, gold, and ivory from Benin, and paid with manillas, cowrie shells, and guns.

Portuguese flag

Ship, called a caravel

British conquest
In 1897, in revenge for an attack on a British party, the British burnt and looted Benin City, exiled the oba, and brought Benin under colonial rule.

Oba Ewuare the Great
The warrior-king Ewuare (r.1440–80) rebuilt Benin City and, under his rule, the surrounding territory reached its greatest extent. Ewuare also established a tradition of secure hereditary successsion.

Ewuare's leopard-shaped arm ornament

Timeline
11th century Benin Empire founded in the forests of Nigeria.

1450 Peak of Benin Empire.

1486 First European to visit Benin is Portuguese explorer, Afonso d'Aveiro; shortly afterward a Benin chief establishes a trading store for the Portuguese.

Benin ornamental sword

1500s English, Dutch, and French merchants start to trade with Benin Empire.

Early to mid-16th century King of Portugal sends Christian missionaries to Benin to convert Oba Esigie, and build churches.

1688 Dutchman Olfert Dapper writes a history of Benin.

1700s Empire weakened by succession struggles.

1897 Britain takes Benin City by force.

1960 Nigeria, including the old Benin Empire, gains independence.

FIND OUT MORE | AFRICA, HISTORY OF | EMPIRES | EXPLORATION | METALS | SONGHAI EMPIRE

B

BICYCLES AND MOTORCYCLES

B

FUN, AND ENVIRONMENTALLY friendly, the bicycle is the simplest form of mechanical transport. A bicycle, or bike, is a two-wheeled machine that converts human energy into propulsion; a motorcycle, or motorbike, is a bicycle with an engine. Modern motorcycles are complex, with engine sizes ranging from 50cc (cubic centimetres) to more than 1,000cc. In many countries, such as China, most people travel or transport goods by bicycle. Across the world, bicycles and motorcycles are used for sport and leisure.

Cannondale SH600, hybrid

Reducing drag

Drag is the resistance of air that can slow down a bicycle or motorcycle and its rider. It is reduced by creating a streamlined shape for the air to flow around – some competitive bicycle riders even shave their legs to achieve this streamlined effect.

Time-trial bike

Parts of a bicycle

From a mountain bike to a racing bike, or a hybrid (a cross between the two), all bicycles are built in a similar way. Designed to be easy to pedal and comfortable, the weight is also important, as it affects the speed at which the bike can be propelled.

Saddles are adjustable, moving up and down to accommodate different riders.

Gears, operated by levers, move the chain between different-sized gear wheels, to change the speed at which the wheels turn.

Handlebars may be dropped for riding crouched.

Brakes are controlled by pulling levers on handlebars, which force brake blocks against wheel rims to slow the bicycle down.

Seat post slides in and out of frame to adjust seat level.

Frame, made from metal tubes, to support the rider.

Brake cable

Chain wheel

Spokes are arranged to create a strong but lightweight wheel.

Tyres fitted on a metal wheel rim give a smooth, quiet ride over small bumps; mountain bikes have fatter tyres to handle rough and rocky terrain.

Pedals, attached to the chain wheel, are pushed to turn the wheel.

Wheel hub secures the wheel to frame.

Parts of a motorcycle

Like a bicycle, a motorcycle has a frame, a rear wheel that drives it along, a front wheel for steering, and controls on the handlebars. Like a car, it has an internal combustion engine and suspension. The suspension supports the motorcycle's body on the wheels, and stops it being affected by the bumping of the wheels on the road.

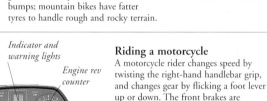

Speedometer

Indicator and warning lights

Ignition switch

Engine rev counter

Motorcycle instrument panel
Motorcycles have an instrument panel in the centre of the handlebars. Control switches for lights and indicators can be operated with hands on the handlebars.

Riding a motorcycle

A motorcycle rider changes speed by twisting the right-hand handlebar grip, and changes gear by flicking a foot lever up or down. The front brakes are operated by hand, and the rear brakes by foot. To go round a corner, the rider turns the handlebars and leans the motorcycle over.

Small engine for speed and economy

Open "step in" frame

SFX moped

Mopeds and scooters
Small motorcycles used for short journeys in towns and cities are called mopeds or scooters. They have small engines, so they cannot go very fast, but are very economical. Mopeds, restricted to a 50cc engine, have pedals which the rider can use on steep hills.

Two-stroke engine with one cylinder. Larger motorcycles have more cylinders.

Lightweight frame

Fuel tank

1992 Yamaha FZR1000 Exup

Three-spoke alloy rear wheel, supported by suspension strut.

Motorcycle tyres grip the road even when the motorcycle leans over at corners. These are smooth, treadless, "slick" racing tyres.

Front suspension

Timeline

1839 Kirkpatrick MacMillan, a Scot, invents a lever-driven bicycle.

1863 The French Michaux brothers build the first pedal-powered bike, a velocipede.

1868 The Michaux brothers add a steam engine to a bike, creating the first motorcycle.

1885 In England, James Starley makes modern-style bicycles.

1885 German Gottlieb Daimler builds an engine-powered tricycle (below).

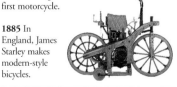

1901 The 1901 Werner is the first practical road-going motorcycle.

1914–18 Motorcycles used extensively in World War I.

1963 Dutchman Van Wijnen designs what will become the Ecocar – covered pedal-powered transport.

| FIND OUT MORE | AIR | CARS AND TRUCKS | ENGINES AND MOTORS | ENERGY | FORCE AND MOTION | MACHINES, SIMPLE | MOTOR SPORTS | POLLUTION | SPORTS | TRANSPORT, HISTORY OF |

Bicycles

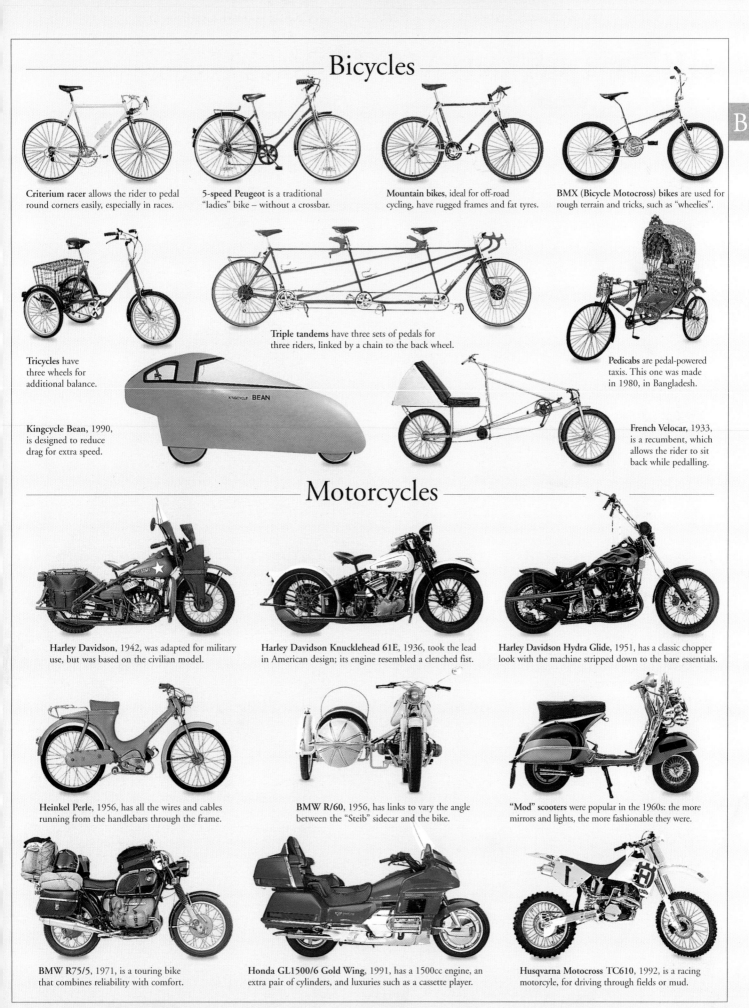

Criterium racer allows the rider to pedal round corners easily, especially in races.

5-speed Peugeot is a traditional "ladies" bike – without a crossbar.

Mountain bikes, ideal for off-road cycling, have rugged frames and fat tyres.

BMX (Bicycle Motocross) bikes are used for rough terrain and tricks, such as "wheelies".

Tricycles have three wheels for additional balance.

Triple tandems have three sets of pedals for three riders, linked by a chain to the back wheel.

Pedicabs are pedal-powered taxis. This one was made in 1980, in Bangladesh.

Kingcycle Bean, 1990, is designed to reduce drag for extra speed.

French Velocar, 1933, is a recumbent, which allows the rider to sit back while pedalling.

Motorcycles

Harley Davidson, 1942, was adapted for military use, but was based on the civilian model.

Harley Davidson Knucklehead 61E, 1936, took the lead in American design; its engine resembled a clenched fist.

Harley Davidson Hydra Glide, 1951, has a classic chopper look with the machine stripped down to the bare essentials.

Heinkel Perle, 1956, has all the wires and cables running from the handlebars through the frame.

BMW R/60, 1956, has links to vary the angle between the "Steib" sidecar and the bike.

"Mod" scooters were popular in the 1960s: the more mirrors and lights, the more fashionable they were.

BMW R75/5, 1971, is a touring bike that combines reliability with comfort.

Honda GL1500/6 Gold Wing, 1991, has a 1500cc engine, an extra pair of cylinders, and luxuries such as a cassette player.

Husqvarna Motocross TC610, 1992, is a racing motorcyle, for driving through fields or mud.

BIG BANG

AN INCREDIBLE EXPLOSION called the Big Bang is believed to have created the Universe. Observations of galaxies and heat radiation from space have helped confirm this theory. Astronomers are now working to explain exactly what happened from the point of the Big Bang explosion which created everything in today's Universe – matter, energy, space, and time – to the present Universe with its galaxies, stars, planets, and us.

Steady State theory

In the late 1940s and the 1950s, the Steady State theory was as popular as the Big Bang theory. It proposed that the Universe looked the same at any place and at any time. Although expanding, it would stay unchanged and in perfect balance. Material was being continuously created to keep the density of the Universe constant. As scientists found proof for the Big Bang, the Steady State theory was largely abandoned.

A Steady-State universe now (left) and later in time (right). The galaxies have moved apart, but new ones (coded orange) have been created to take their place. The density stays the same.

Georges Lemaître

In 1931, Belgian cosmologist Georges Lemaître (1894–1966) was the first to put forward the theory that the Universe started from a dense, single unit of material in a big explosion. The name Big Bang followed in 1950, introduced by Fred Hoyle, a British astronomer and supporter of the Steady State theory.

Origin of the Universe

One of the most difficult problems facing scientists in the 20th century was to explain how the Universe was created. The Universe is changing, but from what and to what? The Steady State theory suggested that the Universe had no beginning or end. The alternative, and now generally accepted, theory is the Big Bang. It proposes that the Universe was created in an explosion 15 billion years ago. From very small and simple beginnings it has grown vast and complex.

At the Big Bang, the Universe is extremely small, bright, dense, and hot.

Seething radiation

Big Bang theory
All matter and time was created in the Big Bang. The explosion started pushing everything away and the Universe has been expanding ever since; and as the Universe expanded, the temperature dropped. A fraction of a second after the explosion, the first tiny particles began to form. By the time the Universe was three minutes old, it consisted of 75 per cent hydrogen and 25 per cent helium. Everything that exists now – galaxies, stars, Earth, and humans – was created from these elements.

Temperature 10,000 trillion trillion degrees. Simple particles form.

Temperature 10 billion degrees. Nuclei of hydrogen and helium form.

Temperature 3,000°C (5,500°F). Clumps of gas form.

Temperature –255°C (–450°F). Quasars, ancestors of galaxies, form.

1 second after Big Bang

3 minutes

300,000 years

1 billion years

3 billion years

Three billion years after the Big Bang, the first galaxies start to take shape. The Milky Way forms 2 billion years later.

Temperature –270°C (–454°F)

The Sun forms inside the Milky Way 10 billion years after the Big Bang. About half a billion years later, Earth is created from leftover material.

Expanding Universe

In the 1920s, analysing starlight from galaxies showed that the galaxies are moving away from Earth. This is true of galaxies in every direction from Earth. Over time, the Universe is becoming larger and less dense. The idea that the Universe started in an explosion from a single point grew out of observations that the Universe is expanding.

Background radiation
The heat produced by the Big Bang has been cooling ever since. It now has a temperature of –270°C (–454°F), detected as microwave radiation from all over the sky. The false-colour map shows variations in the temperature 300,000 years after the Big Bang. The blue (cooler) patches are gas clouds, from which the galaxies formed.

Redshift: The faster a galaxy is moving away, the more the wavelength of its starlight is stretched, or redshifted.

The lines are shifted towards the red end of the spectrum.

More distant galaxies are speeding away faster than closer ones. Their light has a greater redshift.

Lines on the spectrum reveal a galaxy's speed.

Future of the Universe

Nobody knows for certain what is going to happen to the Universe. At present, it is getting larger and less dense. Most astronomers believe there will be a time when it stops expanding. But there is disagreement about what happens then: will the Universe live on for ever, wither and die, or start to contract?

Big Crunch

The Universe may end in a Big Crunch if it starts to contract until it is hot and dense once more. But even this may not mean the end of the Universe. The Big Crunch might be followed by another Big Bang explosion, and the whole process could start over again.

Universe expands after Big Bang.

Universe starts to shrink.

Universe collapses in a Big Crunch.

Second Big Bang

FIND OUT MORE   ASTRONOMY   BLACK HOLES   GALAXIES   GRAVITY   STARS   TIME   UNIVERSE

BIOLOGY

WHEN YOU LOOK at a running horse, you know immediately that it is alive; a beach pebble, by contrast, is non-living. What distinguishes the two is life, or the state of being alive. Biology is the study of life and living things, and it can be divided into two main fields: zoology and botany. People who study biology are known as biologists; the living organisms they study range from animals such as horses to micro-organisms such as green algae. All use energy obtained from food and released by respiration in order to fulfil their natural processes.

Classifying living things

There are around 2 million species of living organisms, and biologists classify them into groups. The largest and most general group is called a kingdom. There are five kingdoms: Monera (bacteria), Protista (protozoa and algae), Fungi, Plantae (plants), and Animalia (animals).

Number of lifeforms in the world

Animalia 1,311,589

Monera 5,500

Protista 65,000

Fungi 81,000

Plantae 400,000

Branches of biology

Biology covers a number of different studies. Ecology examines how living things interact and where they live. Physiology looks at how organisms work. Genetics is concerned with how characteristics inherited from one generation pass to the next. Other branches include anatomy, taxonomy, microbiology, and parasitology.

Bird skeleton

Anatomists study skeletons to understand how an organism functions.

Anatomy
Anatomy is the study of the structure of living organisms. Anatomists investigate the shape and form of the parts that make up organisms. This analysis allows them to work out things such as how bats and birds are able to fly.

Case displays butterflies and moths

Taxonomy
The science of classifying the millions of living things into groups of related organisms is called taxonomy. Scientists called taxonomists identify and name organisms, and then group them together according to the characteristics they share and their common ancestry.

Microbiology
Micro-organisms are living things that are too small to be seen without a microscope. Microbiology is the study of all aspects of the biology of these tiny organisms, which include bacteria, viruses, protists, and some types of fungi such as yeasts.

Compound microscope

Parasitology
Parasites live in or on another organism and exist at its expense; the study of parasites is called parasitology. Fleas are parasites that suck blood from their host. Tapeworms live and feed in their host's intestine.

Magnified flea image

Flea uses needle-like mouth part to suck blood.

Zoology

Zoology is the branch of biology that is concerned with the study of animals. Animals are an amazingly diverse group of living organisms and encompass everything from sponges, spiders, and earthworms to lobsters, cats, and chimpanzees. Zoologists study the structure of animals, how their bodies function, and how they live and behave in their natural environment.

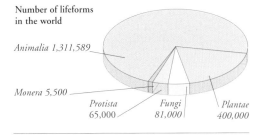

Lorenz

Ducklings imprinted on Lorenz instead of their mother.

Ethology
The study of animal behaviour is called ethology. Austrian zoologist Konrad Lorenz (1903–89) helped establish the science of ethology. He discovered imprinting, a rapid learning process that occurs early in life. Imprinting to food, surroundings, or mother, happens instinctively during a short, fixed timespan early in life.

Kew Gardens, London, England

Work of a biologist
Biologists are trained in all branches of biology, but usually focus on one specific area. Their research might involve observing animal behaviour, investigating plant photosynthesis, or studying ecosystems.

Petri dishes contain control samples.

Biologist at work in a laboratory

Botany

Botany is the study of plants. Plants are diverse organisms, encompassing everything from mosses and ferns to trees, cacti, and flowers. They make their own food by a process called photosynthesis which transforms sunlight into energy. Botanists are concerned with all aspects of the structure, function, and ecology of plants.

Rachel Carson
In 1962, the American marine biologist and writer Rachel Carson (1907–64) published a book called *The Silent Spring*. In it, she warned that the indiscriminate use of pesticides and weedkillers was poisoning the natural world. Her pioneering book was fundamental in starting the environmental movement and in making ecological information accessible to the public.

FIND OUT MORE | ANIMAL BEHAVIOUR | ANIMALS | ECOLOGY AND ECOSYSTEMS | GENETICS | MICROSCOPIC LIFE | PARASITES | PHOTOSYNTHESIS | PLANTS

BIRDS

IN THE LIVING WORLD, only birds, insects, and bats are capable of powered flight. Birds are the largest and fastest of these flying animals, and are the only ones that have feathers. There are about 9,000 species of bird, and they live in a huge range of different habitats – from deserts to the open oceans. They eat a variety of food, which they find mainly by sight. All birds reproduce by laying eggs. Most look after their young until they can fend for themselves.

Wings almost touch during the upstroke.

Pigeon in flight

Fanned tail feathers act as a brake.

Flight feathers are spread out as the bird prepares to land.

Bird features

Birds have a lightweight skeleton and their feathers give them a smooth outline, which helps them move easily through the air. They do not have any teeth, but they have a hard beak instead. Birds use their beaks for eating, and also for many tasks that other animals carry out with their front legs and feet, such as grasping items, or tearing up food.

Feet are held against the body during flight.

Wings
The bones in a bird's wing are similar to those in a human arm. Most birds use their wings to fly. Strong muscles pull the wings downward when the bird flies; other muscles fold them up when not in use.

Legs and feet
A bird's feet and lower legs are usually covered with scales. Muscles that move them are close to the body. The feet are shaped according to their use.

Beak
A bird's beak is covered with keratin – the same substance that makes up human fingernails. The keratin keeps growing so that the edges of the beak do not wear away.

Internal air space with reinforcing struts

Bone structure
Most of the larger bones of a bird are hollow, which saves weight. They contain air spaces that connect to the special air sacs the bird uses when it breathes. Some diving birds have solid bones to make diving easier.

Skeleton
Birds have fewer bones than reptiles or mammals, and many of the bones are fused together. A large flap called the keel sticks out of the breastbone and anchors the muscles that power the wings.

Feathers

Birds use their feathers to fly, and also to keep warm and dry. Each feather is made of fine strands called barbs that carry rows of smaller barbules. In some feathers, the barbules lock together with hooks to produce a smooth surface needed for flying through the air. In others, they stay partly or fully separate. These feathers are soft and fluffy for warmth.

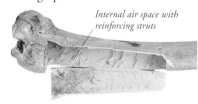

Microscopic hooks lock barbules together.

Macaw flight feather

Curved tip with interlocking barbules

Continuous curved surface

Breeding colours
Male birds often have bright colours which attract mates. In some species, these colours disappear at the end of the breeding season when the birds moult and a new set of feathers grows. In other species, such as pheasants, the colours are permanent.

Central quill

A hollow quill anchors the feather in the bird's skin.

Down feathers
These short fluffy feathers do not have hooked barbs. They form an insulating layer next to a bird's skin. They trap air, which helps to stop heat from escaping from the bird's body.

Body feathers
The tips of these feathers overlap like tiles on a roof, giving the bird a smooth shape. The fluffy base of each feather is close to the body and helps to save heat.

Flight feathers
These feathers are strong but flexible. They provide lift when the bird is airborne. Birds have to preen them carefully to keep them in good condition.

Tail feathers
A bird uses its tail feathers for steering and braking. Some male birds have long or brightly coloured tail feathers. These play an important part in courtship.

Breeding

Birds lay their eggs either directly on the ground or in a nest. One parent – or both – keep the eggs warm by sitting on them, or incubating them. Young birds hatch from eggs at different stages of development. Some can look after themselves almost immediately; others rely on their parents for food and protection.

Eggs
Birds' eggs have a hard shell. Ground-nesting birds often lay eggs that match their background. Birds that nest in trees often lay plain eggs.

Helpless young
Tree-nesting birds usually produce poorly developed young without feathers. The young stay in the nest until they are ready to feed themselves.

Well-developed young
The young of most ground-nesting birds can feed within hours of hatching. They soon leave the nest and follow their mother.

Foster parents
Brood parasites are birds that trick others into raising their young. Here a reed warbler is feeding a cuckoo that hatched in its nest.

B

Vision

Monocular vision
Binocular vision

Owl

Raven

Most birds have a field of view like that of a raven.

Snipe

Blind spot

Vision
Birds that hunt, such as owls, have eyes at the front. This restricts their field of view, but they can judge distances accurately. Shorebirds, such as the snipe, have eyes at the side. They can spot danger in any direction, including behind.

Senses

For most birds, vision is by far the most important sense. It guides them to their food and helps them to avoid their many enemies. Hearing plays a part in helping birds to communicate, and is important to birds that hunt in the dark. The sense of smell is far less vital to birds than it is to many other animals, although some birds, such as the kiwi, use it to find food.

Crane
Like most birds, a crowned crane has keen eyesight. Its eyes are so big that they almost meet in the centre of the skull. Its ear openings are at the base of its crown, but they are hidden by short feathers. Its nostrils are in its beak.

Crown of spiky feathers

Crowned crane

Flight

This complex way of moving requires superb co-ordination. Some birds stay airborne almost entirely by flapping, but others hold their wings out and glide through the air, using the natural curve of their wings to provide lift. During flight, a bird adjusts the shape of its wings to alter its speed and height.

A pigeon's wings allow good manoeuvrability when extended, and fast flight when partly closed.

A kestrel's large wings provide lift as the bird flaps them non-stop while it hovers in the air.

A grouse's wings are shaped for load-bearing rather than speed. A grouse flies only in short bursts.

A peregrine falcon's slender wings partly fold up when it dives out of the sky on to its prey.

Wing shapes
Birds have evolved a variety of wing shapes that enable them to fly in different ways. Some wings provide lots of lift but do not work well at speed. Others create as little friction as possible when they cut through the air, allowing a bird to fly faster.

Flightless birds
During the course of evolution, some birds have given up being able to fly. Flightless birds do not need a light body, and although some are quite small, they include the biggest birds that have ever lived.

Largest and smallest

The world's heaviest bird is the ostrich. It weighs up to 125 kg (275 lb). This is about 80,000 times heavier than the rare bee hummingbird, the smallest bird. This tiny bird's eggs are the size of peas.

The flightless rhea comes from South America.

Feeding and diet

Birds spend much of the time looking for food. To be able to fly, birds need food that provides them with lots of energy. Many of them eat small animals, which they catch either on land, in the air, or in water. Others visit plants and eat fruits, seeds, nectar, and pollen. Some have a mixed diet. Unlike mammals, only a few birds eat grass or the leaves of other plants.

Fish eaters
The great blue heron catches fish by stabbing them with its beak. Other fish eaters snatch their prey with talons, dive-bomb them from above, or chase them through the water.

Seed eaters
Different birds eat different seeds. They usually crack open the seed's husk before eating the food inside. The goldfinch is a typical seed eater. It feeds on thistles.

Insect eaters
Insect-eating birds search for their food on the ground or on plants, or snap it up in mid-air. The goldcrest often feeds high up in trees. Like other small insect eaters, it is expert at spotting insects hidden on leaves or bark.

Meat eaters
Many birds eat small animals, but owls and birds of prey specialize in hunting larger animals, such as mammals, reptiles, and other birds. A hooked beak allows them to tear up their food before swallowing it.

FIND OUT MORE | ANIMAL BEHAVIOUR | BIRDS OF PREY | EGGS | FLIGHT, ANIMAL | FLIGHTLESS BIRDS | NESTS AND BURROWS | OWLS AND NIGHTJARS | SKELETON | SONGBIRDS

Birds

Fish and meat eaters

Large eyes

Black-crowned night heron hunts for fish mainly after dark.

Inca tern flutters in the air before diving down to snatch fish from the surface of the sea.

Spectacled owl has keen eyesight and hearing for catching small animals.

Harris's hawk uses its hooked beak to tear off meat before swallowing it.

Flamingo feeds with its head down, trailing its beak through the water.

Kookaburra is a member of the kingfisher family and feeds in woodland and forests.

Seed eaters

Scarlet eyestripe

African pygmy goose uses its broad beak to collect seeds floating on the water.

Patagonian conure lives in open grasslands of Argentina and Chile.

Mourning dove feeds on the ground in North America.

Eurasian goldfinch has a fine beak and extracts seeds from flowers.

Common waxbill is a common African finch that feeds in open grassland.

Sparrows have short, stout beaks that can crack the husks from small seeds.

Insect eaters

Bushy crest

Kentucky warbler has a narrow beak, ideally shaped for picking up small insects.

Ochre-bellied flycatcher chases after insects and catches them on the wing.

Flycatchers wait on a perch for insects to fly by that they can catch.

Didric cuckoo of Africa specializes in feeding on hairy caterpillars.

Striated yuhina of Asia picks insects off leaves, and often searches under the leaves.

Racquet-tailed roller often feeds on ants and termites from the ground.

Nectar eaters

Bright yellow throat

Blue-crowned hanging parrot has a brush-tipped tongue that helps it to collect nectar and pollen.

Duyvenbode's lory feeds on flowers of New Guinea forest trees, lapping up nectar with its tongue.

Yellow-fronted woodpecker feeds on fruit, probing deep into flowers to reach their nectar.

Rufous hummingbird pumps nectar into its mouth with its tongue.

Booted racquet-tail has quite a short beak, and feeds at flowers with spreading petals.

Fruit eaters

Bill has serrated edges.

Eurasian bullfinch feeds on buds as well as fruit, using its short powerful beak.

Bearded barbet feeds mainly on figs, and uses its heavy bill to dig nest holes in wood.

Chestnut-eared aracari uses its long bill to reach for fruit on the end of long branches.

Fire-tufted barbet of Malaysia eats insects as well as fruit.

Splendid glossy starling gathers in isolated trees that carry ripe fruits.

Long-tailed starling searches for fruit in trees along forest edges.

Mixed food eaters

Eurasian jay feeds on acorns in autumn and winter, but many foods during the rest of the year.

Alpine chough eats small animals and seeds, and also scavenges animal remains.

Blue magpie eats seeds and fruits, and small animals including lizards and snakes.

Swainson's thrush eats insects, spiders, and fruit, particularly in winter.

Red-capped manakin hovers in front of plants to eat the fruit, and also eats insects.

Red-throated ant tanager catches flying insects, and also eats fruit.

BIRDS OF PREY

At the end of a dive, the falcon opens its wings to slow down.

MOST BIRDS OF PREY, INCLUDING EAGLES, hawks, and falcons, kill and eat live animals. They soar high above the ground or dart among trees, using their excellent eyesight to search for their prey. Once they spot a victim, they attack with their sharp talons, then tear up their food with their hooked beaks. Not all birds of prey feed in this way. A few species eat unusual foods, such as snails or nuts. Vultures eat carrion – animals that are already dead. They often wait for another animal to make a kill and then swoop down to the ground to feed on the remains of the carcass.

Long broad wings with finger-like tips

The falcon controls its flight by moving its long wing feathers.

Eyes
Birds of prey have superb eyesight for spotting prey on the ground from high up. Their eyes face forwards, which makes the birds good at judging distances. This is essential for a bird such as the lanner falcon, because it has to know exactly when to brake as it hurtles toward its prey.

Beak
Birds do not have teeth, so they cannot cut meat into pieces before they swallow it. Instead, birds of prey tear up their food with their beaks. Despite the ferocious appearance of a bird of prey's beak, it is hardly ever used as a weapon.

Widely spread flight feathers brake the falcon's flight as it makes an attack.

Bird of prey features
With their forward-facing eyes, sharp claws, or talons, and hooked beak, birds of prey are perfectly adapted for hunting and feeding on meat. Most species have feathers covering the upper legs. These are for warmth and protection.

Lanner falcon
This falcon lives in desert and savannah areas of southern Europe, Africa, and the Middle East. Like other falcons, it catches prey by folding its wings back and falling on it in a steep dive. Falcons also attack birds in mid-air by diving on them from above.

Talons
Birds of prey have large feet with long toes. Each toe ends in a talon, which stays sharp by flaking into a point as it grows. The birds use their talons to kill food, and carry it away. Many species can lift more than half their own weight.

Chukar partridge is prey of the falcon.

Tail feathers are used to steer in flight.

Flying styles
Most large birds of prey, such as eagles, look for food while soaring on currents of rising air. This uses little energy, allowing the birds to fly long distances every day. Smaller species, such as hawks, usually fly in short bursts. Kestrels are unusual in being able to hover in the air.

Splayed feathers reduce air turbulence.

Flight path of kestrel

Kestrel can see small animals on the ground.

Long, narrow wings

Hovering
Kestrels hover close to the ground while looking for prey. This uses a lot of energy, but the kestrels can dive quickly on anything that moves below them.

Flight path of goshawk

Broad, rounded wings

Long, broad wings

Soaring
Eagles, buzzards, and vultures soar by riding on currents of rising air. They spiral around slowly as they soar upwards, keeping their wings straight and steady.

Low-level flight
Hawks usually hunt by flying in short bursts. They are highly manoeuvrable, and can swerve between trees and over hedges, using surprise to catch small birds.

Flight path of eagle

135

B

Roosting
These turkey buzzards from North America have gathered in a tree to roost, or settle for the night. Many vultures roost high in trees or on rocky ledges, because this makes it easier for them to take off and become airborne when the day begins.

Vulture guards carrion while companion eats.

Long neck enables the vulture to reach into a carcass.

Vultures feeding on carrion

White-backed vulture
With a wingspan of more than 2.5 m (8 ft), this huge vulture soars high over open country in southern Europe, Asia, and Africa. Like most other vultures, it has a bare head and neck. If it had long feathers, they would become soaked with blood when it feeds, as it tears the meat from inside a carcass with its beak.

Bare head and neck for ease of cleaning

Carrion eaters
Instead of hunting live animals, vultures feed on the remains of ones that are already dead, carrion. Vultures live in open places, such as deserts, grasslands, and mountains, and find their food by soaring and looking for animal carcasses from the air. Vultures have large beaks, but their talons are weak.

Feeding
Vultures have keen eyesight. If one vulture spots a carcass, and drops down to feed, others quickly follow. Soon vultures arrive from all around. The largest and most dominant species feed first, leaving the smaller species to fight over the scraps.

Specialist eaters
During millions of years of evolution, some birds of prey have developed highly specialized diets as well as specific techniques to deal with their food. Most of these specialist feeders eat animal food, but a few are vegetarians. Some species of bird have learned to live alongside humans, particularly in urban environments, and they eat the variety of food scraps that people throw away.

Egyptian vulture
The Egyptian vulture is one of only a few birds that uses tools to obtain food. It eats ostrich eggs, which it breaks open by picking up stones and hurling them against the shell until it breaks. As well as in Egypt, it lives in other parts of Africa, Europe, and Asia.

Egyptian vulture

Secretary bird

Eyes face to the side instead of the front.

Slim, athletic build for hunting on the ground in open country

Feathery quills, like those once used for writing, give the secretary bird its name.

Lightly built with long wings

Long tail feathers provide balance.

Brightly coloured face

Snail kite
The snail kite lives in marshy places from the southern USA to Argentina in South America. It feeds almost entirely on freshwater snails, which it snatches from the water with one of its feet. It then hooks out the snail's body with its long slender beak.

Snail kite

Palm-nut vulture
The diet of this African vulture is based mainly on the fruits of oil palms, but it eats some small animals. Unlike other vultures, it does not have to fly long distances in search of food, and spends most of its time in trees.

Secretary bird raises its crest of black feathers to attract a mate.

Tough scales protect the legs from poisonous snake bites.

Secretary bird
This highly unusual bird of prey from Africa hunts on the ground. It has long strong legs, and kills animals by stamping them to death. The secretary bird often feeds on snakes, and when attacking uses its wings like a shield to protect itself.

Largest and smallest
The Andean condor is the largest bird of prey, with a wingspan of more than 3 m (10 ft). It is a carrion eater. The smallest birds of prey are pygmy falcons and falconets, which feed mainly on flying insects. Some are only 15 cm (6 in) long.

LANNER FALCON

SCIENTIFIC NAME	*Falco biarmicus*
ORDER	Falconiformes
FAMILY	Falconidae
DISTRIBUTION	Southern Europe, Africa, and the Middle East
HABITAT	Scrub and desert
DIET	Birds, small mammals, and lizards
SIZE	Length, including tail: male – 37 cm (14.5 in); female – 47 cm (18.5 in)
LIFESPAN	About 10 years

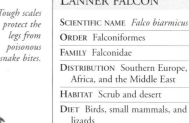

FIND OUT **MORE**

AFRICAN WILDLIFE — BIRDS — DESERT WILDLIFE — FLIGHT, ANIMAL — MOUNTAIN WILDLIFE — OWLS AND NIGHTJARS

Birds of prey
Eagles, hawks, and falcons

Large broad wings

Tail is fanned out to provide lift as the kestrel hovers.

Common kestrel hovers to find its prey, instead of chasing it like other falcons.

Tawny eagle is a scavenger, feeding on carcasses, and even human rubbish. It also steals from other birds of prey.

Goshawk hunts in forests and often catches birds in mid-air.

Black eagle is from southern Asia. It flies over forests and often snatches birds from their nests.

Feathers down to the toes as in all true eagles

American kestrel is a small falcon. It often feeds on insects.

Golden eagle lives in remote places throughout the northern hemisphere.

Harris's hawk sometimes hunts in groups, which is unusual for a bird of prey.

Imperial eagle is rare. It lives in Spain, eastern Europe, and Asia.

Caracara has long legs and toes that enable it to hunt on the ground.

Peregrine falcon is the fastest bird in the world.

Bateleur is almost tailless. This African eagle has an unusual zigzagging flight.

Vultures

Black vulture lives in the Americas. Like the turkey vulture, it has slender legs and toes.

Turkey vulture has an immense range, stretching from Canada to Tierra del Fuego at the tip of South America.

Collar of white feathers around the base of the neck

Huge flight feathers allow effortless soaring.

Worn feathers will be replaced when the vulture moults.

Andean condor is the largest bird of prey. As its name suggests, it lives in the Andes Mountains of South America.

Feet are too weak for catching food.

White-backed vulture has only a few feathers on its neck and a bare head like all vultures.

A bare neck is easy for the vulture to clean after feeding.

BLACK DEATH

B

IN THE 14TH CENTURY, a deadly epidemic swept the world. The Black Death, as it became known, was bubonic plague, a terrible disease that begins with fever, causes agonizing black swellings in the glands, and leads to death, usually within a few days of infection. Millions died. Terrified people fled infected areas and carried the plague with them. In towns the doors of plague carriers were marked with crosses to warn others to keep away. The dead were collected in carts and buried in mass graves. In Europe about one-third of the population died; a similar number probably died in Asia.

Progress of the plague

The plague reached the Black Sea from Asia in 1346. From there, it was carried by Italian traders to ports on the Mediterranean. It then spread up rivers and land routes into northern Europe. By 1350, most of Europe was affected.

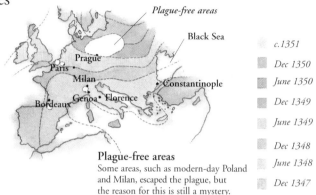

Plague-free areas

Black Sea

Prague
Paris
Milan
Constantinople
Genoa • Florence
Bordeaux

c.1351
Dec 1350
June 1350
Dec 1349
June 1349
Dec 1348
June 1348
Dec 1347

Plague-free areas
Some areas, such as modern-day Poland and Milan, escaped the plague, but the reason for this is still a mystery.

Disease carriers

Plague is caused by a bacterium that lives on rodents. The disease was caught by black rats in Asia, which then colonized ships to Europe and spread the disease among people there. An infected person could also pass the plague through the air, by coughing.

Plague bacterium
The bacterium is called *Yersinia pestis,* after the Swiss biologist Alexander Yersin, who discovered it. It is common in wild animals such as field mice, ground squirrels, and marmots.

Flea carriers
The plague bacterium lives in the digestive system of a flea, and causes a blockage there. When the flea feeds, the blockage makes it vomit the newly eaten blood back onto its host, along with plague bacteria, which then infect the host.

Animal carriers
The black rat lived in towns and on ships and scavenged in food stores and rubbish heaps. Rats carry fleas, and when plague-carrying rats died of the disease, their fleas searched for other hosts. If these new hosts were people, they, too, caught the plague.

Human carriers
The plague turned into an epidemic so rapidly because human travellers helped spread it. Mongol nomads and Asian merchants carried it across Asia. The traders of the great Italian cities, such as Genoa and Venice, carried it around Europe in their ships.

Effects of the plague

The disease was so widespread that many left their families and took to the road to try to escape death. Some thought the plague was God's punishment for the sins of people, and mercilessly whipped themselves in the streets to show repentance.

Labour force
By the end of the 14th century, the smaller population of Europe meant that life was better for those who had survived. Because there were fewer peasants, they got higher wages and there was more food to go around. But recurring peasant rebellions showed that they still had grievances.

20M

8M

Population decline
When Pope Clement VI asked how many people had died from the plague, he was told at least 20 million people in Europe, and 17 million in Asia. In comparison, around 8 million soldiers died in World War I.

Black Death
World War I

= 2 million dead

Dealing with the plague

Some people tried to fend off the plague by using herbal remedies, bleeding by leeches, fumigation, and even bathing in urine. A 14th-century poem, called the Dance of Death (which states that death comes for people of every rank) was often enacted and painted, to remind people that death – and the plague – could strike at any time.

Lungwort   Mint   Rose

Simple lead crosses were placed on corpses in mass graves.

Tombs
During the plague, people faced death every day. Death is often realistically shown on 14th-century tombs, where images of skeletons and decaying corpses are common.

Chantries
People often left money for masses to be said for their souls. These masses were said in special chapels inside churches known as chantries. This chantry is at Winchester, England.

FIND OUT MORE   ASIA, HISTORY OF   DISEASES   EUROPE, HISTORY OF   MEDIEVAL EUROPE   MICROSCOPIC LIFE

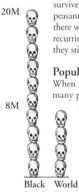

BLACK HOLES

ASTRONOMERS HAVE SPENT much time analysing how stars form and how they develop. One problem was to explain what happened to a massive star at the end of its life. In 1967, the term "black hole" was used to describe one type of object that is left when a massive star dies. Four years later, Cygnus X-1 was found, the first candidate for a black hole.

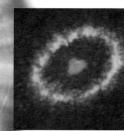

A massive star ends its days in an explosion, leaving a very dense core that then collapses.

Detecting a black hole

Black holes appear black because nothing, not even light, can escape from their powerful gravity. Astronomers cannot detect them directly, but can "see" them because of the effect their gravity has on everything around them, such as gas from a nearby star. The boundary of the black hole is called the event horizon. Material pulled in towards the hole is swirled around by the gravity, forming a disc, before crossing the horizon.

Event horizon

Gravity increases as the core of the dying star shrinks.

Anything trying to escape the gravity must travel almost at the speed of light, as the core approaches the size of the event horizon.

Once the core is smaller than the event horizon, not even light can escape.

The core continues collapsing until it takes up virtually no space. The star is a singularity, a point mass of infinitely high density inside a black hole.

Stellar collapse

Massive stars can end their lives in an explosion, called a supernova, that leaves behind a central core. If the core's mass is more than that of three Suns, it becomes a black hole. Gravity forces the core to collapse. As the core shrinks, its gravity increases. At a certain point it reaches a critical size, that of the event horizon.

Gas is torn from a nearby star.

Close to the black hole, the gas glows with heat.

Black hole

Gravity pulls the gas towards the black hole.

Accretion disc

Event horizon

Gravity
Black holes have incredibly strong gravity which pulls in anything that comes close enough. Anything pulled in beyond the event horizon will be squashed to near infinite density and never escapes.

Accretion disc
The material that swirls around a black hole forms a rapidly spinning accretion disc. As the material is pulled closer to the hole, it travels faster and faster, and becomes very hot from friction. Close to the hole, the material is so hot it emits X-rays before crossing the event horizon and disappearing forever.

Black holes are black because no light or other radiation can escape, and a hole because nothing that crosses the event horizon can get out.

Entering a black hole

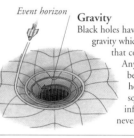

1 At the start of the fall, everything appears normal.

Astronaut becomes distorted.

2 As the astronaut approaches the hole, he starts to be stretched.

3 Light is also stretched to a longer wavelength so the astronaut appears redder.

Galaxy NGC 4261 in the constellation of Virgo has what appears to be a huge accretion disc – 30 million light years across – swirling around a huge black hole.

Supermassive holes

Some galaxies have very active centres that give out large amounts of energy. An object of powerful gravity, such as a supermassive black hole, could be the cause of the activity. Such a hole would be a hundred million times more massive than the Sun.

Inside a black hole

Space and time are highly distorted inside a black hole. Anyone unlucky enough to fall into one would be stretched to resemble spaghetti, as gravity pulled more on the feet than the head. An observer watching the person fall would also see time running slower as the person fell towards the event horizon.

4 Gravity stretches the astronaut. Close to the hole, he is torn apart.

Roger Penrose
The English mathematician Roger Penrose (b. 1931) theorizes on the nature of space and time. He has shown that a massive collapsing star inevitably becomes a black hole, and that all black holes have a singularity – a point, occupying virtually no space, that contains the entire mass of the dead star. Penrose believes the singularity is always hidden by an event horizon.

 FIND OUT MORE   FRICTION   GALAXIES   GRAVITY   STARS   SUN AND SOLAR SYSTEM   UNIVERSE

BOLÍVAR, SIMÓN

SIMÓN BOLÍVAR WAS the brilliant and charismatic leader who led South America to independence from 400 years of foreign rule. Together with other generals, he overthrew the Spanish in just 12 years. As president of the federation of Gran Colombia, he wanted to rule the whole continent, but this dream came to nothing. To this day, he is still known as "The Liberator", and one of the South American nations, Bolivia, is named after him.

Early life

Bolívar was born into a rich family in Caracas, Venezuela, in 1783. His parents died when he was young, and he was educated by private tutors, such as Simón Rodríguez, a teacher who taught him about European ideas, such as liberty.

Fighting for independence

At the start of the 19th century, all of South America, except Brazil and Guiana, was under the rule of the Spanish king Ferdinand VII. Many South Americans resented this and wanted to govern themselves. In response, independence movements broke out all over South America. Bolívar, keen to work in the independence movement, returned to South America and fought the Spanish in Venezuela.

Bolívar's storms to victory at the Battle of Carabobo

Bolívar in Europe
In 1799, Bolívar was sent to Madrid to live with relatives and improve his education. While in Europe, Bolívar learned of an attempt in 1806 by Francisco de Miranda to liberate Venezuela from Spanish rule. The rebellion failed, but inspired Bolívar to fight for independence.

Ferdinand VII of Spain

Angostura Congress
At a congress held at Angostura, now Ciudad Bolívar, Bolívar was elected president of Venezuela. The congress also proposed the formation of Gran Colombia, a federation that included present-day Venezuela, Colombia, Ecuador, and Panama. Between 1819 and 1822, Bolívar won a series of victories against Spain, confirming the independence of Colombia and Venezuela, and liberating Peru.

First republic
In 1810, Francisco de Miranda returned from exile in Europe and was made president of the new republic of Venezuela. In 1811, it became the first South American country to declare independence from foreign rule. Bolívar joined the rebel army, but the republic collapsed. He carried on the struggle, going to Colombia to fight the Spanish there.

Francisco de Miranda in prison

The Liberator
From 1811 onwards, Bolívar was the focus of independence movements across South America. In 1813, he defeated the Spanish and entered Caracas, where he was given the title of "The Liberator". In 1819, he put together an army of 2,500 men and marched them across the continent to Boyacá, Colombia. He won the resulting battle, and Colombia gained its independence.

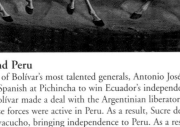

Bolívar and Sucre

Ecuador and Peru
In 1822, one of Bolívar's most talented generals, Antonio José de Sucre, defeated the Spanish at Pichincha to win Ecuador's independence. Two years later, Bolívar made a deal with the Argentinian liberator José de San Martín, whose forces were active in Peru. As a result, Sucre defeated the Spanish at Ayacucho, bringing independence to Peru. As a result of Bolívar's influence, another large area of South America was liberated.

Bolivia

In 1825, Bolívar dispatched Sucre to conquer Alto Perú, in west central South America, which was still under Spanish control. Once the Spanish were defeated, the newly independent country was named Bolivia in honour of the Liberator. By now, every South American state except Uruguay had won its independence.

Bolívar's statue at government buildings, La Paz, Bolivia

SIMÓN BOLÍVAR

1783	Born in Caracas, Venezuela.
1799	Sent to Europe.
1811	Venezuela declares its independence; Bolívar becomes a military leader.
1812	First republic is defeated.
1813	Bolívar enters Caracas as "The Liberator", but is soon defeated.
1819	Angostura Congress.
1819	Bolívar wins Battle of Boyacá to win Colombian independence.
1821	Bolívar wins Battle of Carabobo to win Venezuelan independence.
1822	Ecuador wins independence.
1825	Bolivia named in his honour.
1830	Dies of tuberculosis.

FIND OUT MORE   CENTRAL AMERICA, HISTORY OF   NAPOLEON BONAPARTE   SOUTH AMERICA, HISTORY OF   SPAIN, HISTORY OF

BOLIVIA AND PARAGUAY

BOLIVIA AND PARAGUAY are the only land-locked countries in South America. They are also two of the poorest in the continent, reliant on their neighbours for access to the sea. In a bitter war (1932–35) between them over ownership of the Gran Chaco, Bolivia lost, but both countries suffered political turmoil. Under Spanish rule between the 1530s and 1820s, Bolivia and Paraguay still bear its legacy: Spanish is an official language, and more than 90 per cent of the region's population is Roman Catholic. Many people farm and, in Bolivia, some grow and sell coca for cocaine, a drug that the government has taken steps to banish.

Aymara

The Aymara are a group of native South Americans who have farmed on the Bolivian Altiplano for hundreds of years, strongly resisting cultural change. With the Quechua, another native group, they make up more than half of Bolivia's population, but suffer discrimination and do not contribute to politics or the economy. The state has successfully persuaded many Aymara to move into towns.

Aymara farmers, Altiplano, Bolivia

Physical features

The Altiplano dominates the west of Bolivia, while the east is covered by a lowland plain called the Oriente. Paraguay is divided north to south by the Paraguay River. In the west is the Gran Chaco, a region of grass and scrub; the east is covered in grassy plains and forests, and drained by the mighty Paraná River.

Altiplano

At about 3,800 m (12,467 ft) above sea-level, the Altiplano, a vast, windswept, almost treeless plateau, lies between two ranges of the Bolivian Andes. Despite its cold, arid climate, more than half of Bolivia's population lives here, growing a few crops and rearing animals such as llamas and alpacas.

Lake Titicaca

The clear blue waters of Lake Titicaca cover 8,288 sq km (3,200 sq miles) at a height of 3,810 m (12,500 ft) above sea-level, making it the highest navigable lake in the world. It is the last surviving stretch of an ancient inland sea known as Lago Ballivián.

Gran Chaco

The flat, dry plain that covers southeastern Bolivia and northwest Paraguay is called the Gran Chaco. Since so few people live in this region of coarse grass, thorny shrubs, and cactus, a wide range of plants and animals thrives here.

Regional climate

Bolivia's Altiplano has a cool, crisp, dry climate. The eastern part of the country is warm and humid, as is most of Paraguay. The Chaco is hot, with 50–100 cm (20–40 in) of rain a year, although it often has droughts in winter.

19°C (67°F)   12°C (55°F)

1,890 mm (74 in)

B

Bolivia

The highest and most isolated nation in South America, Bolivia is named after Simón Bolívar, who, in the 1800s, led wars of independence against thc Spaniards. Despite rich natural resources, exporting is difficult because of Bolivia's position. About half the people are Native Americans; the rest are Spanish or of mixed blood.

La Paz
Although Sucre is Bolivia's official capital, the country is governed from La Paz, which also has capital status. At 3,631 m (11,913 ft) above sea-level, La Paz is the world's highest capital and Bolivia's largest city, with a population of about 2,515,000, of whom over half are Native Americans. La Paz has chemical and textile industries, but unemployment is generally high.

Chuqui

Pipes are made from a local reed. The longer the reed, the deeper the sound.

Music
Bolivian music has Incan, Amazonian, Spanish, and African influences. Rural Aymara orchestras are often composed entirely of panpipes, called *chuqui*. Other instruments include drums, flutes, and the *phututu*, made from a cow's horn.

Deforestation
Tropical rainforests in Bolivia are being cut down at the rate of 2,000 sq km (772 sq miles) a year, mostly for cattle ranching or growing coca for cocaine. Chemicals used in the manufacture of cocaine are discharged directly into the rivers of Amazonia, many of which have high pollution levels that damage plant and tree life.

Tin

Metal mining
Bolivia is rich in mineral deposits. Its tin mines lie high in the Andes mountains and it is the world's largest producer of tin. It is also a leading exporter of antimony and silver. Other mineral deposits include zinc, gold, and lead.

BOLIVIA FACTS

CAPITAL CITIES	La Paz, Sucre
AREA	1,098,580 sq km (424,162 sq miles)
POPULATION	8,500,000
MAIN LANGUAGES	Spanish, Quechua, Aymara
MAJOR RELIGION	Christian
CURRENCY	Boliviano

Potatoes

Maize

Barley

Crops
Bolivian farmers living on the Altiplano grow potatoes, soya beans, barley, and wheat for themselves and their families. Rice, maize, bananas, and plantains are grown in the lowlands. Cash crops include sugar-cane, cocoa beans, and coffee, although the profits from illegal coca crops greatly exceed all legal farming produce combined.

Paraguay

The Paraguay River, from which the country takes its name, divides the land in two. To the east lie the fertile hills and plains that are home to 90 per cent of the people. The vast majority are *mestizos*, people of mixed European and Native American ancestry; the rest are Guaraní or Europeans. To the northwest is the Gran Chaco, large areas of which Paraguay won from Bolivia in the 1930s. Only five per cent of the people live in the Chaco, including 10,000 Mennonites, farmers of German descent who retain their culture.

Macá bag

Macá
The Macá are a small ethnic group who follow a traditional lifestyle in the Gran Chaco. They make a living from farming. Macá women also weave bags and cloth for the tourist trade.

PARAGUAY FACTS

CAPITAL CITY	Asunción
AREA	406,750 sq km (157,046 sq miles)
POPULATION	5,600,000
MAIN LANGUAGES	Spanish, Guaraní
MAJOR RELIGION	Christian
CURRENCY	Guaraní

Beef
The main industry in Paraguay's Gran Chaco is cattle ranching. Herds of animals roam the flat grasslands, tended by skilled Paraguayan cowboys called *gauchos* who round the cattle up on horseback. The farms are called *estancias* and are some of the only buildings in this open landscape.

Itaipu Dam
With a reservoir 3,250 sq km (1,255 sq miles) and 220 m (722 ft) deep, the Itaipu Dam, on the Paraná River was undertaken as a joint project with Brazil. It provides water for the world's largest hydroelectric plant and generates enough electricity to make Paraguay self-sufficient in energy.

Dam generates 13,320 megawatts of electricity – enough to supply New York City.

Jesuits
In 1588, Spanish missionaries from the Jesuit order of the Roman Catholic Church arrived in Asunción. They converted the local Guaraní people to Christianity, and taught them trades such as weaving. The Jesuits built large stone churches.

Exports
Soya-bean flour and cotton make up around 50 per cent of Paraguay's exports. The country also sells timber from its forests, vegetable oils, and processed meat. Leading trading partners include Brazil, Argentina, and the Netherlands.

FIND OUT MORE BOLÍVAR, SIMÓN   CHRISTIANITY   DAMS   DRUGS   ENERGY   FARMING   MUSIC   NATIVE AMERICANS   ROCKS AND MINERALS   SOUTH AMERICA, HISTORY OF   TEXTILES AND WEAVING

BOOKS

FROM ENCYCLOPEDIAS TO NOVELS, books are a vital record of human life and achievement. They store the thoughts, beliefs, and experiences of individuals and societies, preserving them after the author's death. There are many kinds of books, from religious works, such as the Qur'an, and non-fiction, such as dictionaries and educational books, to fiction such as plays and stories. The Chinese invented printing in the 9th century; it arrived in Europe during the 15th century. Printing made it possible to mass-produce books, and knowledge was spread more widely. Today, publishing is a global industry.

Early Chinese book, made of fragile bamboo strips

Early books

The first books were not made of paper. Long before 3000 BC, the Sumerians wrote on clay tablets. Around 1300 BC, the Chinese began making books from bamboo strips bound together with cord.

Making books

Much preparation goes into making books and some take several years to produce. For example, making an encyclopedia will involve a team of people that includes authors, editors, designers, picture researchers, illustrators, photographers, and IT experts, as well as printers.

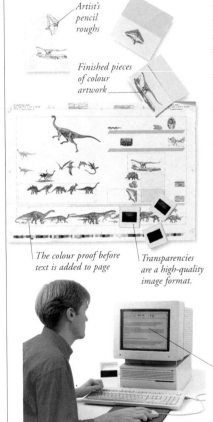

Artist's pencil roughs

Finished pieces of colour artwork

The colour proof before text is added to page

Transparencies are a high-quality image format.

Illustration
The designer draws a detailed plan, showing the position of each illustration. The artist makes rough sketches, which are checked, then paints each picture separately. The artwork is photographed, and carefully positioned on the page using a computer, until the design is perfect.

Author
The author is the first person to start work, researching and writing the contents of the book. The author advises the designer on suitable images for the book and works closely with the editorial team throughout the project.

The printed colour matches the original artwork as closely as possible.

The spine of the book holds the pages in place.

The editor checks the author's text for mistakes and adjusts length of text if necessary.

Text
The text is edited on a computer screen, and then produced as a page called a proof. The proof is matched with the artwork to make sure that words and images fit exactly, before going to the printer.

Finished book
At last the book is finished, and fitted with a hard cover and a protective jacket. It is now ready to sell. An illustrated book may take several years to make, although new technology is speeding up this process.

Pictures and text are perfectly integrated.

Papyrus plants grow by the Nile.

Paper
The ancient Egyptians wrote on scrolls made from papyrus, which grew by the River Nile. Later civilizations in the Middle East wrote on parchment made from animal skin. Modern paper was probably invented in China around AD 150. It was made by pulping flax fibres, then flattening and drying them in the sun. The Chinese kept this process a secret for 500 years before they passed it on to the rest of the world.

CD Roms
There is a limit to how big any book can grow before it becomes too heavy and cumbersome to be practical. Now, modern technology is developing compact alternatives to traditional books. One CD Rom can contain as much text as a shelf of encyclopedias. Text and pictures from CD Roms can be read and transmitted by computer.

CD Rom

Paperbacks
A paperback book contains the same text as a hardback, but has a soft cover. The first modern paperback books were published in London by Penguin, in 1935, priced sixpence. They are far cheaper than hardbacks, and many more people can buy them.

Timeline

c. 285 BC Egyptian pharaoh Ptolemy I establishes a library at Alexandria, Egypt.

AD 300s Books with pages first invented.

Gutenberg Bible

c.1440 Johannes Gutenberg invents the metal type.

1789 French Revolutionaries proclaim the fundamental public right to print without fear of censorship.

1796 Lithography (a technique for printing illustrations) invented.

1811 First totally mechanized printing press invented, USA.

1935 First paperback books published for mass market by Penguin in UK.

1980s Electronic books for the computer published in CD Rom format.

1990s Books first published on the Internet.

FIND OUT MORE   CHILDREN'S LITERATURE   COMPUTERS   DRAMA   EGYPT, ANCIENT   LITERATURE   POETRY   PRINTING   WRITING

BRAIN AND NERVOUS SYSTEM

EVERY THOUGHT YOU HAVE, every emotion you feel, and every action you take is a reflection of the nervous system at work. At the core of the nervous system are the brain and spinal cord, known as the central nervous system (CNS). The most complex part of the CNS is the brain; this constantly receives information from the body, processes it, and sends out instructions telling the body what to do. The CNS communicates with every part of the body through an extensive network of nerves. The nerves and the CNS are both constructed from billions of nerve cells called neurons.

Brain is the body's control and co-ordination centre.

Cranial nerves

aCervical nerves

Brachial plexus

Spinal cord relays information to and from the brain and the rest of the body.

Thoracic nerves

Lumbar nerves

Sacral nerves

Nerves

Nerves form the "wiring" of the nervous system. Each nerve consists of a bundle of neurons (nerve cells) held together by a tough outer sheath. Nerves spread out from the brain and spinal cord and branch repeatedly to reach all parts of the body. Most nerves contain sensory neurons that carry nerve impulses towards the CNS, and motor neurons that carry nerve impulses away from the CNS.

Inside a nerve

Sensory neuron

Motor neuron

Bundle of neurons

Blood vessels

Outer sheath of the nerve

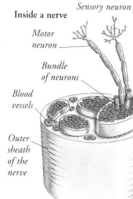

Radial nerve controls the muscles in the arm and hand.

Lumbar plexus

Sacral plexus

Nerve endings

At the ends of sensory neurons there are nerve endings called sensory receptors. If you touch an object, a sensory receptor in the skin is stimulated, nerve impulses travel to the brain along the sensory neuron, and you feel the object. In this way, visually impaired people can "read" the Braille language with their fingertips.

Nervous system

The nervous system is made up of the CNS and the peripheral nervous system, which consists of the nerves. The peripheral nervous system has two sections: the somatic system which controls voluntary actions, and the autonomic nervous system which controls automatic functions such as heart rate.

Sciatic nerve controls the muscles in the leg and foot.

Tibial nerve controls the muscles of the calf and foot.

Neurons

Neurons are long, thin cells adapted to carry electrical signals called nerve impulses. There are three types of neurons: sensory neurons, motor neurons, and association neurons. The most numerous are association neurons, which transmit signals from one neuron to another and are found only inside the CNS.

Synapse

Cell body

Association neuron

Dendrite is a filament that carries signals to cell body.

Cell body

Axon of sensory neuron

aMotor neuron

Sensory neuron

Axon of motor neuron

Neuromuscular junction

Direction of nerve impulse

Touch sensor in skin

Nerve impulses

Nerve impulses are the "messages" that travel at high speed along neurons. Impulses are weak electrical signals that are generated and transmitted by neurons when they are stimulated. The stimulus may come from a sensory nerve ending, or from an adjacent neuron. Nerve impulses travel in one direction along the neuron.

Neuromuscular junction is a synapse between a motor neuron and muscle fibre.

Synapses

A synapse is a junction between two neurons. At a synapse, neurons do not touch. Instead, there is a tiny gap. When a nerve impulse reaches a synapse it triggers the release of chemicals, which travel across the gap and stimulate the second neuron to generate a nerve impulse.

Nerve impulse stimulates muscle fibres to contract.

Reflex actions

If you touch something sharp, you automatically pull your hand away without thinking about it. This is a reflex action. A sensory neuron carries impulses to the spinal cord, where an association neuron transmits impulses to a motor neuron, and the arm muscle contracts.

Brain

Sensory receptors

Motor neuron

Muscle

Receptors in hand detect the prick of a pin and send signal to spinal cord.

Sensory neuron

Santiago Ramón y Cajal

Spanish anatomist Santiago Ramón y Cajal (1852–1934) pioneered the study of the cells that make up the brain and nerves. He developed methods for staining nerve cells so they could be seen clearly under the microscope. His work revolutionized the examination of brain tissue.

Brain

The brain is the body's control centre. Your brain enables you to think and to have a personality, and also regulates all your body processes. It has three main regions: the forebrain, the cerebellum, and the brain stem. The forebrain consists of the cerebrum (which is made up of two halves or hemispheres), the thalamus, hypothalamus, and the limbic system, which controls emotions and instinctive behaviour.

White matter

Grey matter

Section through brain tissue

Grey and white matter

Each cerebral hemisphere has two layers. The outer layer, the cerebral cortex, consists of grey matter containing cell bodies of neurons that form a communication network. The inner layer, or white matter, consists of nerve fibres that link the cerebral cortex to the other parts of the brain.

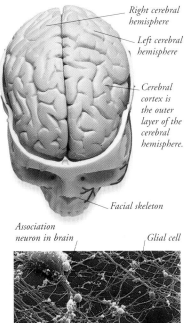

Right cerebral hemisphere

Left cerebral hemisphere

Cerebral cortex is the outer layer of the cerebral hemisphere.

Facial skeleton

Thalamus relays information about the senses to the cerebrum.

Cerebrum is the site of conscious thought.

The two cerebral hemispheres are joined by a band called the corpus callosum.

Hypothalamus regulates body temperature, thirst, and appetite.

Cerebellum co-ordinates movement and balance.

Spinal cord

Frontal lobe

Pituitary gland

Brain stem controls essential automatic functions, such as breathing and heart rate.

Left and right brains

The left cerebral hemisphere controls the right side of the body, and the right cerebral hemisphere controls the left side of the body. Although both hemispheres are used for almost every activity, each hemisphere has its own specialist skills. In most people, the left hemisphere is involved in spoken and written language, mathematical ability, and reasoning, while the right hemisphere controls the appreciation of art and music, insight and imagination, and shape recognition.

Brain cells

The brain consists of hundreds of billions of nerve cells. Many of these are association neurons that are constantly receiving and transmitting nerve impulses. Any one of these neurons can have links to over 1,000 other neurons, producing a complex network. The brain also contains other nerve cells, called glial cells, which hold the neurons in place.

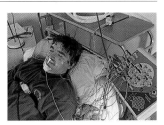

Association neuron in brain

Glial cell

Brain areas

Certain areas of the cerebrum are involved with particular body functions. These areas can be highlighted on a brain map. Motor areas of the brain, such as the speech and basic movement areas, send out instructions to control voluntary movement. Sensory areas, such as the hearing, taste, smell, touch, and vision areas, receive information from sensory receptors around the body. Association areas, such as the frontal lobe, deal with thoughts, personality, and emotions, analyse experiences, and give you consciousness and awareness.

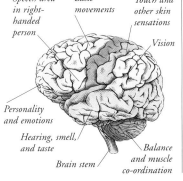

Speech area in right-handed person

Basic movements

Touch and other skin sensations

Vision

Personality and emotions

Hearing, smell, and taste

Brain stem

Balance and muscle co-ordination

Brain waves

The brain's neurons are constantly sending out and receiving nerve impulses. This process produces electrical signals that can be detected using a machine called an electroencephalograph (EEG). Electrodes linked to the EEG can be attached to a person's scalp in order to record the brain's electrical activities as a series of patterns called brain waves.

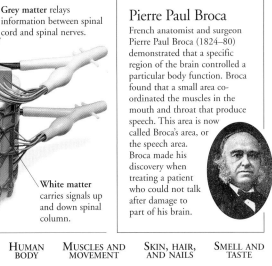

Sleep and dreams

As you sleep, you move repeatedly between phases of light REM (rapid eye movement) sleep and phases of deeper NREM sleep. These shifts can be detected using an EEG.

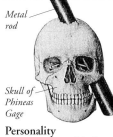

Metal rod

Skull of Phineas Gage

Personality

The frontal lobe of the brain plays a major role in deciding personality. This was shown by the case of an American worker called Phineas Gage. In 1848, an accident sent a metal rod through Gage's cheek and frontal lobe. He survived but his personality changed from being friendly to being aggressive.

Spinal cord

The spinal cord relays information between the brain and the rest of the body, and is involved in many reflex actions. It is a flattened cylinder of nervous tissue, about 43 cm (17 in) long and as thick as a finger. It runs from the base of the brain to the lower back, surrounded by the backbone.

Section of spinal cord

Grey matter relays information between spinal cord and spinal nerves.

Spinal nerve relays nerve impulses to and from all parts of body.

Spinal ganglion

White matter carries signals up and down spinal column.

Pierre Paul Broca

French anatomist and surgeon Pierre Paul Broca (1824–80) demonstrated that a specific region of the brain controlled a particular body function. Broca found that a small area co-ordinated the muscles in the mouth and throat that produce speech. This area is now called Broca's area, or the speech area. Broca made his discovery when treating a patient who could not talk after damage to part of his brain.

FIND OUT MORE   CELLS   EYES AND SEEING   HORMONES AND ENDOCRINE SYSTEM   HUMAN BODY   MUSCLES AND MOVEMENT   SKIN, HAIR, AND NAILS   SMELL AND TASTE

BRAZIL

THE LARGEST COUNTRY in South America, Brazil is a land of opposites. Watered by the second longest river in the world, the Amazon, it has the world's largest rainforest, arid deserts in the northeast, and rolling grassland in the south. Crowded cities contrast with remote areas that have never been explored. The country has many well-developed industries and a huge, successful agricultural base, but many people live in poverty. Brazilian society is a vibrant, diverse mix of cultures.

Physical features

The Amazon Basin and its forests, some mountainous, occupy northern Brazil. The southeast is a region of plateaus that vary from sunburnt arid scrublands to rich fields and pastures.

Highlands
The Brazilian Highlands extend from the Amazon Basin to the coast, rising to 3,000 m (10,000 ft). About 60 per cent of the country is dominated by the plateau, where landscape ranges from tropical forest to dry, rocky desert.

Amazonian rainforest
Around half of Brazil is cloaked in dense rainforest. The River Amazon, 6,448 km (4,007 miles) long, runs through the north of Brazil, giving life to more than 40,000 different species of plants and animals in the forests.

41°C (106°F)   -4°C (25°F)
18°C (64°F)   22°C (72°F)
1,600 mm (63 in)

Climate
All except the extreme south of Brazil lies in the tropics, so temperatures are always high. The Amazonian rainforest receives about 4,000 mm (157 in) every year. By contrast, droughts are common in the northeast corner. Farther south, summers are hot and winters can be cold with frosts.

Brasília
Brazil's modern capital city, Brasília, lies on the extreme northern edge of the plateau region. Purpose-built in the 1950s on the site of a felled rainforest, the city replaced Rio de Janeiro as capital. Its inland position has helped to develop new areas away from the coast. There are many imaginative, futuristic buildings, including the spectacular cathedral.

Brasília Cathedral

Built-up 0.3%   Farmland 10%
Forests 59.5%   Desert 29.7%
Wetland 0.5%

Land use
Thick forests cover the majority of the land, but are being cleared at an alarming rate to make way for farmland and roads. The fertile southeast, especially around São Paulo, is permanently farmed. Much of the land is desert.

B

People

The Brazilian people have a wide ethnic background, and there are large groups of African, European, and Asian origin. The original inhabitants of Brazil form only a tiny percentage of the population. Many families are tight knit, fiercely loyal, and strict Roman Catholics. The majority live in towns clustered along the southeastern coast.

Indian groups
Some native Brazilians still live in the rainforests, following traditional ways of life. However, about 14 groups now shelter in Xingu National Park, set up when their forest home was destroyed.

20 per sq km
(52 per sq mile)

81% **19%**
Urban **Rural**

Leisure

The mainly Roman Catholic people of Brazil celebrate many religious festivals, such as the Rio and Bahía carnivals. Sports, including football, basketball, and water sports along the coast, are the chief leisure activities for millions of Brazilians. The samba, one of the world's most popular dances, originated in Brazil.

Rio Carnival
Known as one of the world's largest and most spectacular festivals, the Rio Carnival, in Rio de Janeiro, is held just before Lent every year. During the carnival, processions of brightly decorated floats, and a myriad of colourful singers, musicians, and dancers with imaginative costumes, fill the streets.

Football
Many Brazilians have a passion for football, either as players or spectators. The national team has won the World Cup more times than any other team. Its star player, Edson Arantes do Nascimento, known as Pelé, was the world's leading player in the 1960s and is regarded by fans as a living legend.

Farming

Brazil has immense natural resources. About 22 per cent of the labour force works on the land, growing all Brazil's own food, with a vast surplus for export. The best farmland is around Rio de Janeiro and São Paulo, where water is plentiful and the climate is frost-free. About 150 million cattle are reared on large ranches in this region.

Cattle ranch, São Paulo

Orange

Coffee leaves and berries

Soya beans

Each berry contains two beans, which are washed, dried, and roasted.

Meat production
Brazil is one of the world's largest producers of beef and veal. Cows graze on the rich, green pastures of central Brazil. Large areas of tropical rainforest are cleared to create new cattle ranches, but the soil is soon exhausted and more forest has to be felled.

Crops
Brazil is a leading producer of cocoa beans, coffee, oranges, and sugar-cane, and one of the world's largest growers of soya beans and bananas. About 22 per cent of the world's coffee comes from Brazil, and millions of oranges are picked every year. These crops grow successfully in the warm, fertile soils of central and southern Brazil.

Bananas

Forest products

The plants and trees of the Amazonian rainforest have long been used for food, housing, and medicine by the people who live there. Some of these, such as rubber and Brazil nuts, are now known world-wide. Other lesser-known plants are quinine, taken from chinchona bark and used to treat malaria; ipecacuanha, an ingredient of cough medicines; and curare, once part of an arrow poison, now a life-saving muscle relaxant used in operations.

Brazil nuts

Transport

A vast network links Brazil's main centres, but of the 1,660,352 km (1,031,693 miles) of roads, only nine per cent are paved. Brazil has one of the world's largest national air networks. Cities with rapid growth, such as São Paulo, are expanding their subways.

Industry

The manufacturing industry employs about 15 per cent of the Brazilian work-force. Machinery, textiles, cars, food products, industrial chemicals, and footwear are the main export products. Brazil has large mining, oil, and steel industries, but has suffered high inflation.

Mining
Brazil is a leading producer of gold, manganese, and tin ore. The country is noted for its precious stones, such as amethysts, diamonds, and topaz, but the quest for mineral wealth has led to much forest destruction.

Steel
South America's top steel maker, Brazil ranks highly in world production. This, and cheap labour, have attracted many car makers to invest in the country.

"Green" cars
About one-third of all Brazil's cars are run on so-called "green petrol", or ethanol, which is made from fermented sugar-cane. Because it produces less carbon monoxide than petrol when it is burned, it is less harmful to the environment and is reducing pollution.

FIND OUT MORE   CHRISTIANITY   CRYSTALS AND GEMS   FARMING   FESTIVALS   FOOTBALL   FORESTS   NATIVE AMERICANS   RIVERS   ROCKS AND MINERALS   SOUTH AMERICA, HISTORY OF

BRIDGES

CURVING MAJESTICALLY across rivers and valleys, bridges are some of the most spectacular structures engineers have ever created. They are also some of the most useful, because bridges can speed up journeys by cutting out ferry crossings, long detours, steep hills, and busy junctions. The first bridges were probably tree trunks laid across streams. Wooden beam bridges and stone or brick arches were the main types of bridge from Roman times until the 18th century, when iron became available to engineers. Most modern bridges are made of steel and concrete, making them both strong and flexible.

Pylon

1 The foundations are laid, and the two pylons are erected. The concrete side spans, which will link the bridge to the shore, are assembled.

Side span

2 The deck sections are hung from cables attached to the pylons, and the bridge begins to stretch across the river from each shore.

Cables

3 The central deck spans are lifted by crane off river barges, welded into place, and attached to cables.

Crane

4 When the last deck section is in place, the bridge is complete. The cables transfer the weight of the deck to the pylons.

Building a bridge

A cable-stay bridge is a type of suspension bridge with a deck hung from slanting cables that are fixed to pylons instead of the ground. Once the pylons are in place, the bridge is built outwards in both directions from each pylon. This ensures that the forces on the pylons balance, so that there is no danger of the pylons collapsing.

Model of the Pont de Normandie

Bridge carries 4 lanes of traffic.

23 pairs of cables attach to either side of pylon.

Pylon of reinforced concrete

Piers support side spans.

Deck is 52 m (170 ft) above water.

Steel cables are coated in plastic to prevent rusting.

Foundations of pylons extend 50–60 m (164–197 ft) below ground.

Types of bridges

On a journey, you may see many different shapes and sizes of bridge, but there are really only a few main types: arch bridges, beam bridges, cantilever bridges, suspension bridges, and cable-stay bridges. The type of bridge used depends on the size of the gap it must span, the landscape, and traffic that will cross it.

Arch bridge
The arch is used to build bridges because it is a strong shape that can bear a lot of weight. To bridge a wide gap, several arches of stone or brick are linked together.

Beam bridge
In a beam bridge, the central span (or beam) is supported at both ends. Very long beams are impractical, because they would be liable to collapse under their own weight.

Cantilever bridge
A beam fixed at one end and stretching out over a gap is a cantilever. Balanced cantilever bridges have several supports, each with two beams that reach out from either side.

Suspension bridge
The deck of a suspension bridge hangs from cables slung over towers and anchored to the ground at each end of the bridge. Such bridges have spans of up to 1 km (0.62 miles).

Isambard Kingdom Brunel

English engineer Isambard Kingdom Brunel (1806–59) was a genius of bridge design. Brunel designed and built two of the earliest suspension bridges. He also planned and built railways and several huge steamships.

Aqueducts

Not all bridges carry roads or railway tracks. An aqueduct is a bridge that carries water. The Romans built aqueducts to supply water to the baths and drinking fountains in their cities. More recent aqueducts carry canals over steep-sided valleys in order to keep the canal level. This avoids having to build long flights of locks.

Aqueduct on the River Dee, Wales

Timeline

200 BC Roman engineers build arch bridges of stone or wood, and aqueducts.

1779 The first bridge made of cast iron is built at Ironbridge, England.

1883 In the USA, New York's Brooklyn Bridge is the first bridge to be supported by steel suspension cables.

1930 Switzerland's Salginatobel Bridge is constructed of reinforced concrete (concrete strengthened with steel).

Sydney Harbour Bridge, Australia

1932 Australia's Sydney Harbour Bridge opens, carrying a road and rail tracks suspended from a huge steel arch.

1998 The Akashi Kaikyo suspension bridge over Japan's Akashi Strait has the longest main span in the world.

 FIND OUT MORE BUILDING AND CONSTRUCTION | IRON AND STEEL | RIVERS | ROADS | ROMAN EMPIRE | SHIPS AND BOATS | TRAINS AND RAILWAYS | TRANSPORT, HISTORY OF | TUNNELS

BRONTË SISTERS

THREE OF THE FINEST writers of the 19th century, Charlotte, Anne, and Emily Brontë, were brought up in solitude in a small town in northern England. In spite of many difficulties, including being far away from the world of publishing in London, they produced some of the most popular novels of the period. The books portrayed characters with a new frankness and showed how difficult life could be for women of that era. Their stories still enthral readers of today.

Haworth parsonage

The Brontë sisters were brought up in the small town of Haworth in Yorkshire, northern England. Their father was the curate (priest) at the local church, so they lived at the parsonage (clergyman's house). It was a grim stone building, with a view over the graveyard.

Brontë family
Charlotte, Emily, and Anne lived with their father, Patrick Brontë and their brother, Branwell. Their mother, Maria, died when the children were young and two other children died in infancy, so the sisters were brought up by their aunt. They had a lonely life. They mixed little with other children and had to make their own entertainment.

Education

Charlotte and Emily were sent away to Cowan Bridge school. The conditions were poor and made Charlotte ill. Lowood school, in *Jane Eyre*, is based on her time there. All three sisters later worked as teachers, or governesses – one of the few jobs then open to educated young women.

Manuscripts are still preserved at Haworth parsonage.

Cowan Bridge school

Poetry manuscript by Charlotte Brontë at around the age of 14

Manuscripts and illustrations completed by the Brontë sisters in their teenage years.

Novelists

In 1846, the Brontës started to get their works published. They began with a volume of poems, but only two copies were sold. In the following two years Emily's *Wuthering Heights*, Charlotte's *Jane Eyre*, and Anne's *Agnes Grey* were published. At the time it was not thought proper for the daughters of clergymen to write fiction, so the sisters used pseudonyms (false names), to keep their identities secret. Many people bought the books and wanted to know more about the authors.

Bell brothers
The Brontë sisters published their books under three male names – Acton, Currer, and Ellis Bell, the initials of which matched those of the sisters' own names. To begin with, even their publishers did not know who the "Bell brothers" really were.

WUTHERING HEIGHTS

A NOVEL.

BY
ELLIS BELL.

IN THREE VOLUMES.

VOL. II.

LONDON:
THOMAS CAUTLEY NEWBY, PUBLISHER,
72, MORTIMER St., CAVENDISH Sq.
1847.

Jane Eyre
Charlotte Brontë's first novel tells the story of Jane Eyre and her struggle to be an independent woman in a hostile society. Working as a governess, she falls in love with her employer, Mr Rochester, only to discover terrible secrets in his past. The novel was considered radical in its time.

Wuthering Heights
Emily Brontë's novel follows a series of tragic relationships through different generations and is especially famous for its depiction of Catherine and Heathcliff. Set against the Yorkshire countryside, the novel deals with contemporary issues of social change and industrialization.

Angria and Gondal

To amuse themselves in the bleak moorland rectory, the Brontë children invented two imaginary lands, called Angria and Gondal. They wrote many stories and poems about these lands, which were peopled with heroes and heroines who lived exciting and tragic lives.

CHARLOTTE BRONTË

1816 Born Yorkshire, England.

1822–32 Educated at Cowan Bridge School and Miss Wooler's School, Roe Head, Yorkshire.

1846 Publishes her poems.

1847 Publishes *Jane Eyre*.

1849 Publishes *Shirley*.

1853 Publishes *Villette*.

1854 Marries Arthur Nicholls.

1855 Dies.

FIND OUT MORE   BOOKS   CHRISTIANITY   DICKENS, CHARLES   FILMS AND FILM-MAKING   LITERATURE   UNITED KINGDOM, HISTORY OF   WRITING

BRONZE AGE

IN ABOUT 3000 BC, prehistoric people began to use bronze – an alloy of copper and tin – instead of stone, to make weapons and ornaments. The dates for this development, which is known as the Bronze Age, vary from culture to culture, but the earliest bronze workers probably lived in Mesopotamia (modern Iraq). These people initially used pure gold and copper, which were easy to hammer into shape, before discovering how to make bronze. They were also responsible for developing the world's first civilizations. The Bronze Age was followed by a time when people learned to smelt and shape iron ore to produce stronger tools and weapons. This period is known as the Iron Age.

Stone wristguard with gold screws

Copper dagger blade

The first metalworkers

In the early days of the Bronze Age, metalworkers used gold, copper, and bronze for luxury items, or for high-status weapons, such as the dagger in the Barnack grave, England. People still made tools from stone, because stone was harder than bronze.

Pottery beaker for use in the afterlife

The Barnack grave, c.1800 BC

Prongs for lifting meat from a cauldron

Flesh hook

Copper
The royal family of the city of Ur in Mesopotamia used copper for jewellery, as well as for everyday items, such as this flesh hook. They used gold to make beautiful vessels for special occasions.

Making bronze

People learned how to extract metal from ores by heating the rock. The metal could then be used to make useful or decorative objects.

Ore
This common type of copper ore was fairly easy for people to spot on the ground.

Yellow chalcopyrite

Blue bornite

Smelting
To extract the metal, Bronze Age people heated the ore to a high temperature. When the metal in the ore reached melting point, they collected it in a round, stone crucible.

Casting

Bronze Age people cast objects by pouring hot, molten bronze into a mould. When the metal had cooled and set, the mould was opened, revealing the finished item. Casting was used to produce decorative items.

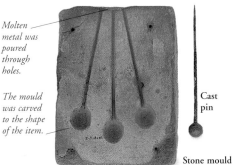

Molten metal was poured through holes.

The mould was carved to the shape of the item.

Stone mould

Cast pin

Mould
This is one half of a stone mould for casting pins. It was made in Switzerland, c.1000 BC. To use the mould, the two halves were fastened together, and metal poured in through the holes at the top.

Cast pin
Bronze pins like this were cast in the stone mould. The mould used to make this pin was carved to create the delicate pattern on the pin-head.

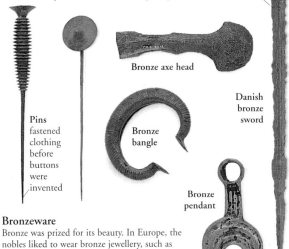

Ornate French sword

Bronze swords were sometimes cast, although they were stronger when the bronze was beaten into shape. This Danish sword is polished to show the original golden colour of bronze.

Bronze axe head

Pins fastened clothing before buttons were invented

Bronze bangle

Danish bronze sword

Bronze pendant

Bronzeware
Bronze was prized for its beauty. In Europe, the nobles liked to wear bronze jewellery, such as bangles and pendants, and bronze pins in their clothing. Bronze swords were high-status weapons.

Trace of an ingot

Ingots
Early metalworkers discovered how to add molten tin to copper to make bronze. Liquid bronze was poured into round moulds and left to set. The blocks of bronze were called ingots.

Timeline
3800 BC The earliest known metal objects are produced by smelting. Copper is the main metal smelted in Tepe Yahya, Iran.

3000 BC Bronze objects are used throughout western Asia, where copper is being combined with tin.

2500 BC Bronze is used in the cities of Mohenjo-Daro and Harappa, Indus Valley.

2000 BC Bronze-working comes to the civilizations of the Minoans on Crete and the Myceneans in mainland Greece. These Aegean cultures trade in Europe for copper and tin.

1900 BC Iron Age starts in western Asian areas such as Turkey, Iran, and Iraq.

1800 BC Bronze Age reaches European areas, such as modern Slovakia.

Shaft-tube axe, Hungary

800 BC Early Iron Age starts in central Europe.

FIND OUT MORE   GREECE, ANCIENT   INDUS VALLEY CIVILIZATION   METALS   MINOANS   POTTERY AND CERAMICS   STONE AGE   SUMERIANS

BUDDHA

BUDDHISM IS A WORLD faith that has changed the lives of millions of people. It began in Sakya, a small kingdom in northeast India. The founder of Buddhism was a prince, called Siddhartha Gautama, but today he is known simply as the Buddha, a title meaning "the enlightened one". When he was a young man, Siddhartha began a search for an understanding of suffering. By the end of his life he had become the Buddha, founded the Buddhist faith and already had many followers.

Early life
According to tradition, Siddhartha was born while his mother, Maya, was on her way to visit her parents. She died soon afterwards. His father was told that the boy would become either a great ruler or a Buddha. The king was afraid that Siddhartha would leave the court to become a holy beggar, so confined him to the palace grounds. But eventually he left to search for the true meaning of suffering.

Siddhartha, later called the Buddha

Maya, mother of the Buddha

The Buddha meditating

Buddha sat under a holy fig or bo tree

Enlightenment
When Siddhartha left the palace, the suffering he saw around him made him decide to become a holy man. He spent six years depriving himself of food and sleep, and learning about spiritual matters. Eventually he realized that this made him too weak for deep reflection, so he meditated under a tree. Here he made the breakthrough to an understanding of the truth known as enlightenment.

Teaching
After experiencing enlightenment, the Buddha set out to teach others what he had learned. Many were converted, and the Buddha sent them away as wandering missionaries. Later, the Buddha returned to his father's court to teach his own people what he had learned. His father was among the first to be converted.

Sarnath
At Sarnath, near Varanasi, the Buddha preached his first sermon to five men who had previously sought enlightenment with him. He taught them that suffering is caused by desire, and to end suffering they must give up desire. Sarnath became the site of one of the greatest Buddhist shrines.

Mara, the demon

Buddha

Temptations
While Siddhartha was meditating, a demon named Mara sent his beautiful daughters to tempt him from his chosen path. Mara also whipped up a storm and hurled thunderbolts at Siddhartha. But the young man carried on meditating, unmoved. He meditated for a whole night before understanding the truth, which he called *dharma*, and reaching peace, or *nirvana*, in his heart.

Buddha

Bimbisara
Even during his own lifetime, the Buddha commanded so much respect that many people left their homes to follow him and form orders of monks and nuns. When King Bimbisara gave the Buddha a generous gift of land – "the gift of the bamboo grove" – Buddha's followers built the first Buddhist monastery there.

King Bimbisara

THE BUDDHA
Earliest records of Buddha's life were written more than 200 years after he died, so details are hard to verify. The following dates are accepted by most authorities.

563 BC Siddhartha Gautama, son of King Suddhodana of the Sakya, born in northeast India.

533 BC Siddhartha leaves his father's court to become a holy man.

527 BC Siddhartha attains enlightenment, and becomes the Buddha.

483 BC Buddha dies at Kusinagara, in Oudh, India.

Death of Buddha

Pilgrim

Later life
When the Buddha was 80 years old, he ate some food that had been accidentally poisoned, and died at Kusinagara in India amongst his disciples. Many people came to pay homage to him. His body was cremated and the remaining bones were placed under stone mounds that have since became holy places of pilgrimage for Buddhists.

FIND OUT MORE	BUDDHISM	CHINA	INDIA, HISTORY OF	MAURYAN EMPIRE	MONASTERIES	SHRINES

BUDDHISM

THE BUDDHIST FAITH was founded by an Indian nobleman called Gautama Siddhartha in the 6th century BC. Gautama, who became known as the Buddha, or the "Awakened One", told people how to achieve fulfilment. He taught that fulfilment is reached by meditation, wisdom, and correct behaviour in all aspects of life. Buddhists also believe in reincarnation, in other words that a person can be reborn after death. The Buddha is revered by his followers, but not worshipped as a god. For this reason, Buddhism exists side-by-side with other religions in many countries. There are probably some 320 million Buddhists worldwide, although the majority are in Asia.

Rites and ceremonies

Ceremonies at Buddhist temples are usually simple. They involve reciting extracts from Buddhist scriptures and making offerings to the Buddha. A monk may give a sermon. Some Buddhist rituals also involve candle-lit processions and music-making. The Buddhist year is enlivened with festivals, most of which take place at full Moon. The most famous festival is Wesak, at New Year, which celebrates the birth, enlightenment, and death of the Buddha.

Hand gestures on a statue of the Buddha

The Buddha touches earth as witness to his worthiness for Buddhahood.

This gesture shows the Buddha actively turning the Wheel of Law.

The Buddha reassures an approaching person.

The Buddha

Statues of the Buddha are kept in temples and homes to inspire Buddhists to live as he did. Buddhists bow before the statue to show their respect. They also carry out the ceremony called "Going for refuge", in which they recite texts that show their dedication to the Buddha, to his teaching (the Dharma), and to the community of Buddhists (the Sangha).

Teachings

The Buddha taught the Four Noble Truths, which explain the Buddhist attitude to suffering and how fulfilment can be achieved. The Truths say that suffering is always present in the world; that the human search for pleasure is the source of suffering; that it is possible to be free from these desires by achieving a state called nirvana; and that the way to nirvana is through the Eightfold Path.

Wheel of Law

Pictures in the inner circle reveal the six realms of existence.

In each realm, a Buddha-figure helps the beings there.

Three animals in the centre are symbols of ignorance.

Wheel of Life

The Eightfold Path
The Path teaches that the way Buddhists lead their lives should be correct in eight important aspects: understanding, thought, speech, action, means of livelihood (work), effort, recollection, and meditation. The eight-spoked Wheel of Law shown above represents each of the eight stages of the Path.

Karma
Buddhists believe in the law of karma. According to this law, good and bad actions result in fitting rewards and punishments, both in this life and in later rebirths. The Wheel of Life is a symbol of rebirth. When people die, they are reborn into one of its six realms of existence.

Offerings
Buddhists regularly make offerings to the Buddha, such as flowers and food. Burning incense or candles and scattering petals around the Buddha's statue are ways of making an offering that also beautifies the temple. The light of the candles is the light of the Buddha's great wisdom, and the smoke from incense wafts the truth of the doctrine towards the devotees.

The Buddha's topknot is a sign of his princely wisdom.

His face has the serene expression of meditation.

Long ear lobes symbolize his nobility.

Eyes cast down show that he is meditating.

Coloured sash is changed for each season.

Candles

Incense

Lotus flowers

Meditation
Buddhists meditate in order to purify their minds and free themselves from thoughts about material things. In this way they hope to achieve "perfect mindfulness", one of the stages in the Eightfold Path. One way in which they meditate is to concentrate on feeling their breath going in and out. This empties the mind of selfish thoughts, making the person calmer and the mind clearer.

Buddha's cross-legged position is called the lotus position.

Branches of Buddhism

From its beginnings in India, Buddhism spread around eastern and Southeast Asia, where the majority of the world's Buddhists still live. There are also Buddhist communities in other parts of Asia, and in the West. Buddhism has two main strands – Mahayana and Theravada – but other forms of Buddhism with distinctive features have also developed.

Theravada

This branch of Buddhism is closest to the teachings of the Buddha himself. It is dominant in Southeast Asia (Burma, Cambodia, Laos, Sri Lanka, and Thailand). Theravada Buddhists revere the Buddha and do not worship other figures. They aim to become "perfected saints" by following the Eightfold Path and tend to believe that people can reach the state of nirvana only through their own efforts.

Mahayana

This form of Buddhism prevails in China, Korea, Japan, Mongolia, Nepal, and Tibet. A follower's first aim is to become a Bodhisattva, an enlightened being who does not pass into nirvana but remains in this world in order to help others to enlightenment. Mahayana Buddhists therefore place a high value on charity.

Monks are given offerings of food by locals.

Almsgiving emphasizes the close relationship between monks and lay people.

Chinese Bodhisattva head

Zen

This form of Buddhism originated in China and spread to Japan in about the 13th century. Zen Buddhists aim to lead a simple life, close to nature, using everyday actions as a means of meditation. Zen Buddhists meditate in a way that tries to see beyond logical patterns of thought and preconceived ideas.

A Zen monk tidies a garden.

Tibetan Buddhism

A form of Mahayana Buddhism is found in Tibet. Here, special value is placed on the Buddhist virtues of meditation and wisdom. Tibetan Buddhists have their own rituals, such as repeating sacred sayings, or mantras. Since the Chinese invasion of Tibet in the 1950s, few Buddhist monasteries remain in Tibet.

Mantra

Inside a prayer wheel is a mantra that the monk repeats while spinning the wheel.

Monasticism

Buddhist monasteries began when the Buddha's followers built permanent settlements to live in together during the rainy season. Today there are many monks (and some nuns) who devote their lives to explaining the Buddha's teachings and setting an example by the way they lead their lives.

The monk's meditative pose suggests peace and stability.

Shaven head shows the monk has renounced worldly vanities.

Sharpening stone

Alms bowl lid is also used as a plate.

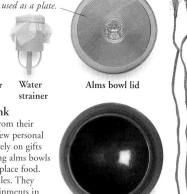

Needle and thread **Razor** **Water strainer**

Alms bowl lid

Living as a monk

Monks live apart from their families and have few personal possessions. They rely on gifts for survival, carrying alms bowls into which people place food. They obey strict rules. They must avoid entertainments in which there is singing or dancing, give up decorative clothes, and eat only at set times.

Alms bowl **Belt or girdle**

Sacred texts

Buddhism has sacred texts made up of sayings and sermons, many of them attributed to the Buddha. One of the most important books of writings is the Dharmapada, which forms part of the Pali Canon, the oldest collection of Buddhist scriptures.

In Tibetan-style libraries, manuscripts are wrapped in cloth and placed between boards.

Library in Shey Monastery, Ladakh, India

Temples

The religious buildings of Buddhism vary widely in their shape and decoration, from Japanese pagodas to Thai wats. But all contain statues of the Buddha. The statues act as a focus for devotion and for offerings. People go to the temples to carry out acts of private worship and for special ceremonies.

Wat Benchamabophit, in Thailand's capital, Bangkok, is known as the marble temple.

Stepped roofs symbolize stages of spiritual development.

Devotees gather with their offerings in the grounds of the temple.

Dalai Lama

The Dalai Lama is the spiritual and political leader of Buddhists in Tibet, who believe that each Dalai Lama is a reincarnation of the previous one. The present Dalai Lama, Tenzin Gyatso, was born in 1935. In exile since 1959 following the Chinese takeover, he is still Tibet's most important leader.

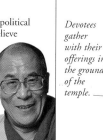

FIND OUT MORE   ASIA, HISTORY OF   BUDDHA   CHINA, HISTORY OF   FESTIVALS   MAURYAN EMPIRE   RELIGIONS   SHRINES   SIGNS AND SYMBOLS   THAILAND AND BURMA

BUFFALO AND OTHER WILD CATTLE

THE FIVE SPECIES OF BUFFALO, and all other cattle, are members of the family Bovidae. They have split, or cloven, hooves, and both sexes have horns which they can use to defend themselves. The animals also gain some protection from living together in herds. Only the anoas are solitary animals. Cattle were among the earliest animals to be domesticated. The Asiatic buffalo, yak, banteng, and gaur all have a domesticated version. Loss of habitat, hunting, and diseases have drastically reduced the world's wild cattle. No fewer than nine of the eleven species are in danger of extinction.

Broad hooves support the weight of the buffalo.

Bison

Plains bison

Often wrongly called buffalo, there are two species of bison. The American bison is a grass-land animal which appears in two forms – the plains bison and the woods bison. The European bison, or wisent, is a forest dweller. Bison are massive animals standing more than 1.5 m (5 ft) tall and weighing more than 910 kg (2,000 lb).

American bison
The head, neck, and forequarters of the American bison are covered with long hair, which, with the large hump, makes the forequarters appear much bigger than the hindquarters. The horns are short and curved, and are grown by both sexes.

European bison
The wisent lives in Poland's Bialowieza Forest. It is taller than the American bison and has a longer, less barrel-like body, and longer legs. Its hindquarters are also more powerfully built.

African buffalo

The buffalo is the only species of wild cattle found in Africa. Cape buffalo bulls are up to 1.5 m (5 ft) at the shoulder and weigh more than 816 kg (1,800 lb). Their horns have a span of up to 1.5 m (5 ft) and form a massive helmet, or boss, across the head. A smaller sub-species, the forest buffalo, lives in equatorial forests.

Asiatic buffalo
There are four species of Asiatic buffalo – the water buffalo (shown here), the lowland and mountain anoa, and the tamarau. The water buffalo occurs in a domestic and a wild form, but only a few wild herds survive. Its horns are semi-circular and sweep outward and backward.

Endangered tamarau

Confined to the highlands on the island of Mindoro in the Philippines, this dwarf buffalo has been relentlessly hunted. Only about 100 survive today.

Largest and smallest
Wild cattle range in size from the wild yak, which is more than 2 m (6.5 ft) high at the shoulder, to the mountain anoa, which is no more than 76 cm (30 in) high.

Mountain anoa

Wild yak

Oxen

The group of wild cattle commonly called oxen contains four species – the yak, the banteng, the gaur, and the kouprey. Domestic cattle also belong to this group. Most breeds of domestic cattle are descended from the now-extinct aurochs, which at one time inhabited the plains and woodlands of Europe and Asia in great numbers.

Yak
Largest of the wild cattle, the wild yak lives in herds high up on the Tibetan Plateau in Central Asia. To protect them against the bitterly cold climate, yaks have long, shaggy black hair reaching almost to the ground, with a thick undercoat.

Banteng
Found in Southeast Asia, Java, and Borneo, the banteng is a shy animal. Females and young are a brick-red colour; adult males are black.

CAPE BUFFALO

SCIENTIFIC NAME	*Syncerus caffer*
ORDER	Artiodactyla
FAMILY	Bovidae
DISTRIBUTION	Africa, south of the Sahara
HABITAT	Grassland and woodland savannahs, but seldom far from water
DIET	Mainly grass, occasionally supplemented with foliage
SIZE	1.5 m (5 ft) at the shoulder
LIFESPAN	About 20 years

FIND OUT MORE

DEER AND ANTELOPES   FARMING   NORTH AMERICAN WILDLIFE   SHEEP AND GOATS

BUGS

THE WORD BUG is often used to describe any crawling insect or a disease-causing germ. The true bugs are a group of insects that have long feeding tubes specially adapted for sucking fluids out of plants and animals. Bugs, such as shield bugs, are often brightly coloured, and, as a group, they are remarkably varied in shape. There are about 55,000 species of bug, including large solitary insects, such as giant water bugs and cicadas, and tiny creatures, such as scale insects, bedbugs, and aphids. It is the smaller bugs, such as greenfly and leaf hoppers, that create problems for farmers because of the severe damage they cause to crops.

Features of a bug

All bugs have specialized mouthparts with cutting implements for piercing, and needle-like sucking tubes held within a protective sheath. Some bugs, such as lantern bugs, have their membranous wings exposed when at rest; others have forewings that are partially thickened and used not for flight, but as a protective cover for the delicate hind wings.

Lantern bug, with wings open

False eyes

Extension to head

True eyes

Abdomen

Two sets of wings

Forewings overlap at rest.

Jointed legs

Spines on hind legs are used for defence.

Lantern bug

Reproduction

Bugs attract a mate in many ways, such as giving off scent, or vibrating the surface of water. Male cicadas attract females with their loud song, produced by drum-like organs on the abdomen. During mating, male and female bugs are often attached for hours. Females usually lay hundreds of eggs. These hatch into nymphs – tiny versions of their parents – and moult many times before reaching adult size.

Parthenogenesis

Aphids such as greenfly and blackfly, multiply rapidly, because they can reproduce without mating. Females produce a succession of identical female offspring from unfertilized eggs, each of which later produces more of the same. This is called parthenogenesis.

Shield bugs

Shield bugs are found virtually worldwide. They are also called stink bugs, as they can give off a bad smell. Females protect their eggs and young from attack.

Young shield bug nymphs being guarded by their mother.

Feeding

Bugs use their mouthparts to cut a hole in their food and pierce the soft parts inside. They inject enzymes and digestive juices through a pair of tiny tubes to break down solids and suck up the resulting fluids. In this way, predatory bugs, such as assassin bugs, can suck their victims dry. Bedbugs are parasites that suck the blood of birds and mammals, including humans. Some bugs feed only on plant juices.

Assassin bugs

Assassin bugs are carnivores. Most prey on other invertebrates, such as millipedes. Some steal prey already caught in spiders' webs. Assassin bugs can squirt toxic saliva at would-be predators.

Feeding tube

Assassin bug feeding on a cockroach.

Leaf hoppers

Leaf hoppers are herbivores. They are often considered pests as they cut holes in the leaves of plants, such as cotton plants, to suck out the sap, thereby weakening the plants.

Defence

Small bugs face many enemies from ladybirds to birds. To deter would-be attackers, bugs have evolved a range of defences. Some bugs, such as tree hoppers, have developed elaborate camouflage; others, such as stink bugs, give off bad smells. The larvae of spittle bugs, also known as frog hoppers, hide within a frothy substance called cuckoo spit. Aphids employ ants to protect them by providing their guardians with a nutritious sugary secretion.

Tree hoppers

Tree hoppers camouflage themselves with projections of cuticle that resemble thorns.

Water bugs

Some bugs live in water. Pond skaters skim over water on their dainty legs, while water boatmen dart below the water using paddle-shaped limbs. Underwater bugs come to the surface to breathe, or carry around an air bubble.

Pond skater

RED-BANDED LEAF HOPPER

SCIENTIFIC NAME	*Graphocephala coccinea*
ORDER	Homoptera
FAMILY	Cicadellidae
DISTRIBUTION	Eastern USA and eastern Canada
HABITAT	Meadows and gardens
DIET	Plant juices
SIZE	Length 8–11 mm (0.4–0.5 in); wingspan 12–16 mm (0.5–0.6 in)
LIFESPAN	Adults: up to 4 months

FIND OUT MORE ARTHROPODS · CAMOUFLAGE AND COLOUR · FARMING · FLIGHT, ANIMAL · INSECTS · LAKE AND RIVER WILDLIFE · PARASITES · PLANTS, DEFENCE

BUILDING AND CONSTRUCTION

THE SIMPLEST BUILDING is a permanent structure with a roof and four walls. Buildings come in a huge variety of shapes, sizes, and appearances – from skyscrapers and factories to schools, hospitals, houses, and garden sheds. Despite these differences, all buildings have the same basic purpose – to provide a sheltered area in which people can live, work, or store belongings. The engineers, surveyors, and construction workers who plan and build these structures also work on other projects, such as roads, bridges, dams, and tunnels.

Early building
Since the beginning of history, people have built shelters to protect themselves from the weather, wild animals, and their enemies. The first buildings were simple, single-storey structures made of materials such as wood, stone, and dried grass and mud. The first large-scale stone constructions were temples for the worship of gods and goddesses, and palaces in which powerful leaders lived. About 6,000 years ago, people discovered how to bake clay bricks. In time, engineers developed new building methods that enabled them to build higher and lighter structures.

Walls are made from mud and bricks dried in the Sun's heat.

Ancient tower-house, Sana, Yemen

Anatomy of a building

Most buildings have certain features in common, such as walls, a roof, and floors. A large modern building, such as this airport terminal, also has a strong internal frame. Underneath this are the solid foundations on which the whole structure rests. The building is equipped with services, such as electricity and water supplies, as well as escalators, stairs, or elevators to give access to different storeys, and fire escapes that enable people to leave the building rapidly in the event of an emergency.

Roof
A roof is a protective covering over a building. Roofing materials include thatch, clay tiles, slate, glass, and steel. Roofs in wet climates are shaped to make rainwater run off; in cold countries, they slope steeply to stop snow from building up; and in dry climates, they are often flat. Sloping roofs are held up by supports called roof trusses.

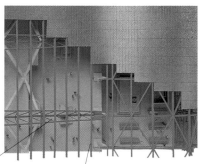

Roof trusses sit on frame.   *Roof truss*

Steel beams | **Overhead cutaway of roof**

Kansai Airport, Japan

Glass wall lets in a lot of light.

Roof is clad with shiny steel panels.

Floor rests on columns, which are part of frame.

Foundations
A building's foundations spread its huge load evenly into the ground, stopping the building from sinking under its own weight. Pile foundations are columns that rest on hard rock; raft foundations are concrete platforms that rest on soft rock. The foundations form the base on which the building's frame is constructed.

Internal frame
The "skeleton" of a large building is its internal frame, which supports the roof, the walls, and the floors. Frames can be made of wood, steel, or reinforced-concrete columns and beams joined together.

Foundations extend underground.

Basement houses service machinery.

Walls and floors
In a house, the walls – which may be made of wood, stone, or brick – are strong enough to hold up the floors, ceilings, and roof trusses. In a larger structure, however, the frame supports the building's weight, and the walls simply hang from the frame. The floors in a large modern building are reinforced-concrete slabs.

Structural engineers

Long before the construction of a building is underway, structural engineers begin working on the design of the building with an architect. They calculate how strong the building's structure needs to be and draw up detailed plans, usually on a computer. When the building work commences, they make sure that everything happens safely, on time, and within the financial budget.

Structural engineer on a building site

Surveyors
Accuracy is extremely important in construction work if the completed building is to have vertical sides and level walls, and be structurally safe. Even small errors in the design or assembly can result in parts not fitting together properly. People called surveyors check the building at every stage of its construction, using special instruments, such as theodolites and spirit levels, to take accurate measurements.

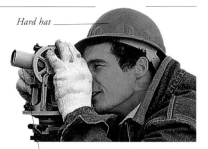

Hard hat

Theodolite is an instrument that measures angles to find distances, lengths, and heights.

Surveyor using theodolite

Building sites

The different stages in the construction of a large building must always take place in a certain order, starting with the preparation of the site. Materials and machinery must arrive just when they are needed: if they are too early, the site may get too crowded; if they are too late, the building work may be delayed.

Site clearance and excavation
The building site must first be cleared, which may involve demolishing other buildings, removing vegetation, and leveling the site. Holes are excavated (dug) for the foundations and basement.

Foundation laying
The next stage is to build the foundations. This involves driving steel beams, called piles, into the ground, or pouring liquid concrete into a deep pit to form a solid base that will support the building.

Frame building
The building's frame soon rises from the foundations. The frame is built either by bolting together steel beams, or by pouring concrete into molds crossed by steel rods. A shell of metal poles and wooden planks, called scaffolding, is temporarily erected around the building so that workers can reach all parts.

Completed building is ready for use.

Completion
With the frame in place, work starts on the floors, walls, and roof. Services such as water and waste pipes, heating and air-conditioning ducts, and electricity and telephone cables are installed on each story. Finally, the windows are inserted, and the interior is decorated.

Equipment

Some of the tasks on a building site, such as plastering a wall or laying bricks, are done by tradespeople using hand tools. Other tasks, such as erecting the building's frame or lifting heavy objects, may require large, specialized machines. Together, these machines are known as construction plant.

Plumb line

Set square

Spirit level

Trowel

Bricklayer's tools

Hand tools
Each tradesperson involved in building and construction uses special tools. A bricklayer, for example, uses a trowel to spread mortar onto bricks, a plumb line to ensure that a wall is vertical, and a spirit level and a set square to check that it is horizontal.

Construction plant
Powerful machines, such as cranes and cement mixers, can do jobs in a few minutes that would take manual workers hours or even days. Other machines include pile-drivers to hammer steel piles into the ground, bulldozers to level building sites, and excavating diggers.

Backhoe digger

Trench-digging bucket

Hydraulic jacks steady digger.

Wide shovel tool scoops up soil.

Building materials

Some building materials, such as steel, concrete, and bricks, are structural – that is, they make up the basic structure of the building. Other materials, such as ceramics and glass, are mainly decorative. Traditional materials, such as stone and wood, have been used for many centuries and are often found locally.

Building site materials

Steel rods for reinforced concrete

Wooden planks for scaffolding

Steel girders for frame

Concrete and steel
Most modern buildings contain concrete, steel, or a combination of both. Concrete is a mixture of cement, water, and small stones (called aggregate) that hardens like rock when it sets. Steel is iron that contains a tiny amount of carbon. Concrete strengthened by steel rods is called reinforced concrete.

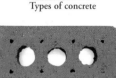

Types of concrete

Wood
Some houses have floors made of wooden planks and wooden beams for roof trusses. Scaffolding may have walkways of wooden planks.

Bricks
Blocks of hardened clay, called bricks, are laid in rows and joined together with mortar – a mixture of cement and sand.

Local materials
Many buildings throughout the world are built from materials that occur naturally in the surrounding area. These local materials may include straw, mud, stone, wood, and even animal dung. They can do just as good a job as modern manufactured materials, which are usually more expensive and have to be imported from elsewhere.

Decorative wooden battens

Thatch is made of interlaced bundles of straw (dried grass or reeds).

Reeds

Metal rods secure bundles.

Cutaway of a thatched roof

Straw

Construction workers
People from a wide range of trades with many different skills will work on a building before it is finished. These tradespeople include welders, bricklayers, electricians, carpenters, plasterers, and plumbers. For safety reasons, construction workers often wear hard hats and other protective clothing, such as goggles.

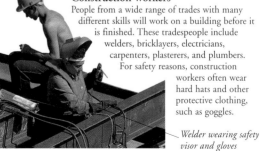

Welder wearing safety visor and gloves

FIND OUT MORE   ARCHITECTURE   BRIDGES   CHURCHES AND CATHEDRALS   DAMS   HOUSES AND HOMES   IRON AND STEEL   ROADS   TUNNELS

BUTTERFLIES AND MOTHS

SCALY WINGS AND A COILED feeding tube set butterflies and moths apart from other insects. Together, they form a single group of about 170,000 species, of which 90 per cent are moths. Both have four stages to their life cycle in which they change from a caterpillar to an adult with wings. They feed on plants, and rely on camouflage, irritating hairs or spines, or poisons in their body for protection against predators.

Scales overlap like the tiles on a roof.

Wing scales
Scales on the wings contain coloured pigments. Some scales produce colours by reflecting the light.

The front and back wings of a moth are hooked together.

Moth's bright colouring indicates it is poisonous

Zygaenid moth

Moths

Most moths fly at night. They tend to have drab colours, and have a fatter body and longer, narrower wings than butterflies. When resting, moths usually hold their wings open or fold them flat over their back.

Proboscis is rolled up when not in use.

Moth antennae have a large surface area for picking up scents.

Feeding tube
Adult butterflies and moths suck up liquid food, such as flower nectar, through a tube called a proboscis. A few moths have no proboscis because they do not feed as adults.

Antennae
Insects use their antennae for smelling, touching, and tasting. Butterfly antennae are clubbed; moth antennae range from single strands to feathery branches.

Swallowtail butterfly

Butterflies

In most cases, butterflies are more brightly coloured than moths and have a thinner body. Unlike moths, they hold their wings upright when resting. The front and back wings are loosely joined together by a lobe on the back wing that grips the front wing. Butterflies are usually active by day rather than by night.

Wings are made of a tough membrane supported by a network of rigid veins.

Life cycle
Butterflies and moths start life as an egg, which hatches into a caterpillar. This feeds and grows until it turns into a pupa. The adult develops inside the pupa. This process of change is called metamorphosis.

Pupa protects developing adult.

Adult butterfly emerges.

Butterfly pumps blood into its wings to expand and stiffen them.

Adult Blue Morpho

Henry Bates
Henry Walter Bates (1825–92) was a British naturalist and explorer who studied camouflage in animals. He found that some harmless insects look the same as a poisonous insect so that predators leave them alone. This is now called Batesian mimicry, after Henry Bates.

Defence

To escape from predators, butterflies and moths often fly away or hide. Some have irritating hairs or spines, or are poisonous. Bright colours may warn predators that a butterfly or moth is poisonous. Poisons often build up in a caterpillar from the plant it eats. These then remain in the adult.

Camouflage
Many butterflies and moths blend in with their surroundings at some stage of their life cycle. Camouflaged like this, they may escape predators.

Eyespots
False eyes on the wings can startle predators or stop them from pecking the real eyes. A damaged wing is not as serious as an injury to the head.

Mimicry
Some butterflies and moths gain protection by looking like another species of butterfly or moth. The top butterfly shown here is poisonous; the bottom one is not.

Wing colour
When a butterfly is resting, only the underside of its wings shows. This is often coloured for camouflage. The colours of the upper side help to attract a mate.

SWALLOWTAIL BUTTERFLY

SCIENTIFIC NAME *Papilio palinurus*

ORDER Lepidoptera

FAMILY Papilionidae

DISTRIBUTION From Burma to the islands of Borneo and the Philippines in Southeast Asia

HABITAT Tropical rainforest

DIET Flower nectar

SIZE Wing span: 9.5 cm (3.75 in)

LIFESPAN Varies (The adults of most butterflies live for only a few weeks or months)

 FIND OUT MORE

CAMOUFLAGE AND COLOUR

INSECTS

FLIGHT, ANIMAL

Butterflies

Owl butterfly

Japanese emperor

Brown-veined white

Orange-barred giant sulphur

Great spangled fritillary

Viceroy

Common opal

Great orange tip

Common blue

Peacock

African giant swallowtail

Small copper

Blue morpho

Chequered skipper

Swallowtail

Cairns birdwing

Hewitson's blue hairstreak

Moths

African moon moth

Goat moth

Buff-tip

Provence burnet moth

Magpie moth

Owl moth

Hornet moth

Hoop pine moth

Garden tiger

Giant agrippa

Verdant sphinx

Oak eggar

Madagascan sunset moth

Pale tussock

Hieroglyphic moth

BYZANTINE EMPIRE

IN 395, THE GREAT ROMAN EMPIRE split into eastern and western sections. The western half – still called the Roman Empire – was centred on Rome. The eastern half became the Byzantine Empire with its centre at Constantinople. The Greek character – in language, customs, and dress – of Constantinople contrasted with Latin Rome. Despite efforts on the part of emperors to reunite the two halves of the old empire, the Byzantine Empire gradually grew away from Rome. The Roman Empire collapsed in 410, but the Byzantine Empire existed until 1453 when the Ottoman Turks captured it.

Extent of Byzantine Empire, c.565
Because of its fabulous wealth, superb shipbuilding facilities, and strategic position between Asia and Europe, the Byzantine Empire was under almost constant siege by its powerful neighbours – Persia, Arabia, Turkey, and some states of the Christian west.

Mosque

Byzantium to Constantinople
The ancient Greek port of Byzantium stood on the Golden Horn, a strip of land surrounded by sea on three sides. Constantine the Great (c.274–337) re-designed the city and re-named it Constantinople in 330 AD. Soon it was one of the world's most beautiful cities.

Bridge over the Bosporus Strait, linking Asia and Europe

East versus west
By the 9th century, the Byzantine form of Christianity was changing from the western, or Roman, form. Greek had replaced Latin as the official language, and the Roman pope and Byzantine patriarch argued over church ritual. However, they were united in their fear and hatred of the non-Christian Turks and Arabs.

Great Schism
In 1054, representatives of the Roman and Byzantine churches excommunicated each other. This religious split, or schism, destabilized political links between east and west, and caused mutual suspicion and hostility.

Orthodox priest

Art and religion
Byzantine churches were famous for their interiors, which were lavishly decorated on a huge scale, with painted icons and intricate mosaic images of Christ, the Virgin, and saints.

Icons
In the 8th century, the empire was racked by arguments over whether it was idolatrous to worship beautiful religious statues and paintings, known as icons. Finally in 843, it was declared to be legitimate, and their production increased. Later, icons were portable, and collected by Renaissance artists.

St Gregory of Nazianzus *Virgin and Child* *St John Chrysostom*

Triptych icon, 12th century

Gilt covering

Hagia Sophia
The biggest church in the eastern empire, Hagia Sophia was built in only five years (532–37). The Ottomans converted it into a mosque in the 16th century, and today it is a museum.

Fall of Constantinople
Constantinople was conquered twice: once by the west and once by the east. In 1204, it was ransacked by Christians on their way to the Holy Land. In 1453, Ottoman Turks overran it, and it became a Muslim stronghold.

Fall of Constantinople, 1453

Mosaics
Byzantine artists pressed cubes of tinted glass, marble, or precious stones into beeswax or lime plaster to make a mosaic. Artists often decorated the images with gold and silver leaf.

Christ Pantokrator, 11th century

Timeline

395 Roman Empire divided into west (Roman) and east (Byzantine).

867–1056 Empire reaches its peak.

The Good Shepherd mosaic, 5th century

529–34 Justinian I introduces his Roman Law Code.

976–1025 Basil II, known as "the Bulgar-slayer", gains more land than any emperor since Justinian I.

1054 Great Schism: Byzantine church breaks with the Roman church and forms the Eastern Orthodox church.

1096 First Crusade: European army joins Byzantine army at Constantinople.

1204 Fourth Crusaders sack Constantinople.

1453 Ottoman Turks capture Constantinople, ending the empire.

Emperor Justinian I
Justinian I (r.527–565), expanded the empire in the west by conquering North Africa, southern Spain, and Italy, while holding off the Persian threat in the east. In addition Justinian built Hagia Sophia, and his Codex Justinianus, or Roman Law Code, still forms the basis of the legal system in many European countries.

FIND OUT MORE

ART, HISTORY OF   CHRISTIANITY   OTTOMAN EMPIRE   PERSIAN EMPIRES   ROMAN EMPIRE

CAESAR, JULIUS

JULIUS CAESAR WAS A BRILLIANT general and ruler of the Roman world. He is one of the most famous, and controversial, figures in history. He transformed the Roman world, expanding Rome's territory into Gaul and suppressing many revolts. He was a fine administrator, reforming the Roman calendar and Roman law and bringing strong government to the republic. Caesar was also a great writer and orator. But he could be unscrupulous in pursuit of his own interests, and made many enemies during his career.

Early life
Caesar was born in Rome in about 100 BC. A member of a rich family, he had a successful military and political career, rising through various offices to become Pontifex Maximus, or high priest, in 64 BC. In 61 BC he became Governor of Further Spain, one of the most important jobs in the Roman republic.

Triumvirate

In the years leading up to 60 BC, rival politicians competed to gain power. Order was restored when Caesar, the financier Marcus Crassus, and the army commander Pompey set up a three-man committee, or triumvirate, to rule Rome. In 59 BC, the triumvirate allowed Caesar to be elected consul, one of the two magistrates who held supreme power. As consul, Caesar strengthened and reformed the government.

Pompey
Gnaeus Pompeius Magnus (106–48 BC), known in English as Pompey, was a Roman general who conquered Palestine and Syria, and did much to get rid of opposition to Roman rule in Spain and Sicily. Although he was a member of the triumvirate and he married Caesar's daughter, he was always Caesar's rival.

Pompey the Great

Gallic wars

From 58–50 BC, Caesar waged a series of wars which led to the incorporation of Gaul (modern France and Belgium) into the Roman republic. Caesar displayed great military ability in the Gallic Wars, and was ruthless with any tribes who tried to resist conquest. Caesar recorded his achievements in his famous memoirs of the campaign.

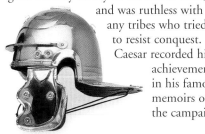

Roman legionary's helmet

Civil war

After the death of Crassus in 53 BC, rivalry between Caesar and Pompey reached new heights. Pompey became sole consul in 52 BC and, with the support of the Roman senate (parliament), declared Caesar an enemy of the people. In 49 BC, Caesar crossed the Rubicon, the river dividing Italy from Gaul, and marched on Rome in triumph. In 48 BC he defeated Pompey. By 45 BC, Caesar had removed all opposition, becoming master of the Roman world.

Roman catapult bolts

Roman cavalry spur

Cleopatra
Caesar followed Pompey to Egypt and remained in the country after Pompey's death. He befriended and lived with Cleopatra, queen of Egypt, and helped establish her firmly on the throne. When Caesar returned to Rome in 47 BC, Cleopatra came with him. After Caesar's death, the Egyptian queen had twin sons with the Roman soldier and politician Mark Antony (c.82–30 BC).

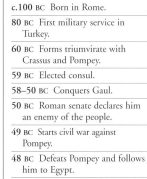

Antony and Cleopatra

Caesar as soldier

Caesar crosses the Rubicon.

Pharsalus
Caesar showed his military skills when, in 48 BC, he defeated the much larger army of Pompey near the Greek town of Pharsalus. Caesar's strategic sense and better location enabled his small force to overwhelm Pompey's army, which was routed. Pompey himself fled to Egypt, where he died.

Battle of Pharsalus

Dictator

In 45 BC, Caesar was appointed dictator for life. He reformed the living conditions of the Roman people by passing new agricultural laws and improving housing. He also made the republic more secure from its enemies.

Assassination
Despite his reforms, Caesar's dictatorial rule made him enemies in Rome. On 15 March 44 BC – the Ides of March – Caesar was stabbed to death in the senate house by rival senators, including Cassius and Brutus. But his work lived on in his great-nephew and adopted son, Octavian, who became emperor.

Assassination of Caesar

JULIUS CAESAR

c.100 BC	Born in Rome.
80 BC	First military service in Turkey.
60 BC	Forms triumvirate with Crassus and Pompey.
59 BC	Elected consul.
58–50 BC	Conquers Gaul.
50 BC	Roman senate declares him an enemy of the people.
49 BC	Starts civil war against Pompey.
48 BC	Defeats Pompey and follows him to Egypt.
44 BC	Assassinated in the senate in Rome by rival senators.

FIND OUT MORE   ARMIES   FRANCE, HISTORY OF   ITALY, HISTORY OF   ROMAN EMPIRE   UNITED KINGDOM, HISTORY OF

CAMELS

WELL-SUITED TO DESERT LIFE, camels can withstand extreme conditions. There are two main types: the one-humped dromedary, which lives in Africa and Arabia, and is usually domesticated; and the two-humped Asian Bactrian, some of which still roam wild in the Gobi Desert. Closely related to camels are four animals without humps – llamas, alpacas, guanacos, and vicunas. All six species, called camelids, belong to the artiodactyls, a group of herbivorous, even-toed mammals that also includes cattle.

Features of a camel

Camels are the largest of the even-toed mammals, standing up to 2.4 m (8 ft) at the shoulder. They have long legs, and walk at an ambling pace. Camels have a split upper lip, which allows them to eat dry, spiky plants. Their lips and upright heads have given camels a reputation for arrogance. In reality this is nonsense. However, camels may spit at, or bite, humans if annoyed or frightened. During the mating season, male camels often fight, biting their rivals when competing for females.

Hump
Contrary to popular belief, the camel's hump is not filled with water, but is a fat store that provides the camel with energy when food is scarce. Because fat is stored in the hump, there is less fat under the rest of the skin enabling the camel to lose heat more easily in hot conditions.

Long eye lashes

Slit-like nostrils

Split upper lip

Head of dromedary camel

Eyes and nostrils
Camels have long eyelashes that protect their eyes from fierce sandstorms and enable them to see under difficult conditions. They can close their slit-like nostrils to reduce the amount of sand and dust blowing up the nose, and minimize moisture loss from the nasal cavity.

Thick fur keeps camel warm during cold desert nights, and helps prevent overheating in the day.

Feet
Camels' feet have two toes joined by a web of skin; underneath is a soft, flexible pad that splays out when the camel walks. The camel's feet are very wide, and this, together with the pad, prevents the camel from sinking into soft sand and enables it to walk over rough terrain.

Web of skin

Large, wide feet with soft pads allow camel to walk on sand.

Foot of dromedary

Shaggy fur

Bactrian camel

Long legs help camel walk long distances.

Dromedary camel

Long, curved neck, allows camel to reach desert vegetation.

Ships of the desert
Camels are the only animals that can carry heavy loads long distances in extreme heat and with little water. Nomadic peoples survive in deserts by using camels as pack animals, as well as for meat, milk, and skins.

Salt-laden caravan, Taoudenni, Mali

Water loss
Camels can exist for long periods without water, but make up the loss quickly when water is available. Camels are also adapted to reduce water loss by producing dry faeces and small amounts of syrupy urine. In addition, their body temperature can rise to 40.5°C (104.9°F) during the day, reducing the need to keep cool by sweating, a process that also causes water loss.

During long periods without drinking, a camel can lose 40 per cent of its body mass as water.

Within 10 minutes, camels can drink sufficient water to make up huge losses.

Types of camelid
Related to camels are two species of domesticated camelid, the llama and alpaca, and two wild species, the vicuna and guanaco; all live in or near the Andes mountains in South America. Small herds of guanaco feed on grass and shrubs in shrubland and savannah up to heights of 4,250 m (13,900 ft), from southern Peru to southern Argentina.

Vicunas are a protected species.

Alpacas' wool may be black, brown, or white.

The wool, milk, and meat of llamas are all used.

Vicuna
Vicunas, the smallest of the camelids, live in family groups at high altitudes.

Alpaca
The highland peoples of Peru and Bolivia breed alpacas for their long, soft wool.

Llama
Llamas are used as pack animals to carry loads of up to 100 kg (220 lb), at altitudes of 5,000 m (16,400 ft) over long distances.

DROMEDARY CAMEL

SCIENTIFIC NAME	*Camelus dromedarius*
ORDER	Artiodactyla
FAMILY	Camelidae
DISTRIBUTION	Domesticated in North Africa, Middle East, southwestern Asia; feral populations in Australia
HABITAT	Desert
DIET	Any type of desert vegetation, including thorny twigs and salty plants that other animals avoid
SIZE	Head and body length 3 m (10 ft); shoulder height 2 m (6.5 ft); weight up to 600 kg (1,320 lb)
LIFESPAN	Up to 50 years

 FIND OUT MORE

| ANIMALS | ASIAN WILDLIFE | DESERTS | DESERT WILDLIFE | MAMMALS | PIGS AND PECCARIES | SOUTH AMERICAN WILDLIFE |

CAMERAS

A LIGHTPROOF BOX with a hole or lens at one end, and a strip of light-sensitive film at the other, is the basic component of a traditional camera. To take a photograph, the photographer points the camera at an object and presses a button. This button very briefly opens a shutter behind the lens. Light reflected from the object passes through the lens and on to traditional film or a digital chip to produce an image.

Shutter release button · Shutter and film speed dial · FM2 · Self-timer lever · Lens · Lens release button

Shutter and film speed dial · Connection for flash · Film rewind knob · Shutter release button · Aperture scale · Distance scale · Lens

Parts of a camera

The quality of a photograph is controlled by adjusting the film and shutter speed dials, flash, and aperture scales. This is because the final image will depend on the type of film in the camera, the amount of light that enters the lens, and the length of time that the film is exposed to light.

35mm cameras
The most popular cameras are the 35mm, named after the width of the film they use. These cameras are small and easy to manage. They often have in-built features, which adjust automatically to variations in light and distance, to ensure that a clear photograph is taken every time.

Digital cameras

Digital cameras contain no film. Instead, the image is captured on a photosensitive chip. Photos are displayed instantly on a screen on the camera and can be deleted if not liked. Images can be loaded into a computer and printed out.

Computer imaging
After an image has been stored on a digital camera, it can then be fed into a computer. From here it is printed out on photo paper or sent over the Internet. Special software allows the picture to be manipulated and gives the photographer a lot of control over the image.

Images are set to high or low quality.

Some cameras can also record tiny video clips.

Cyber-shot 2.1 MEGA PIXELS

Digital camera

Batteries inside supply power.

Flashes

Movable flash head · Flash light sensor

A flash provides the extra light needed for taking pictures after dark, or in dim conditions. The flash is electronically controlled to go off at the moment the shutter opens.

A mirror sends light from the lens to the viewfinder while the shutter is closed.

Light enters the lens

Single-lens reflex camera
Unlike other cameras, the view through a single-lens reflex (SLR) camera is that of the actual image that is recorded on the film. Mirrors in the viewfinder correct the upside-down image sent from the lens.

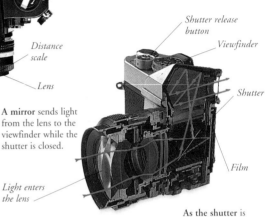

Shutter release button · Viewfinder · Shutter · Film

As the shutter is released, the mirror slips up allowing the light to reach the film (shown by the dotted line).

Lenses

Different lenses achieve different visual effects. A wide-angle lens allows more of the scene to appear in a photograph than a normal lens. A telephoto zoom lens can take a close-up shot of a distant object. The fisheye lens distorts images for dramatic effect. These lenses are detachable from the camera.

Normal lens · Telephoto zoom lens · Wide-angle lens · Fisheye lens

Film types

Today, plastic film comes in various sizes and speeds, in a colour or a black and white format, packaged as rolls or plates. The speed, given in ASA/ISO or DIN numbers, indicates how quickly the film reacts to light. A new device, the Electronic Film System, fits into a 35mm camera and holds up to 30 digital images which can be transferred to a computer.

AGFA 110mm film · AGFA 35mm film · Plate film

George Eastman

An American inventor, George Eastman (1854–1932), formed the Kodak company. In 1884, he produced the first roll film and in 1888 the first box camera, making photography an accessible hobby. In 1889, he used clear celluloid film on which the first movie pictures were taken.

Timeline

4th century BC The "camera obscura" is developed; it consists of a darkened room into which an image is projected.

1822 Frenchman Joseph Niepce takes the first photograph on a sheet of pewter, coated with bitumen.

1839 Niepce's colleague, Louis Daguerre, announces process for recording images on copper.

1839 William Fox Talbot, an Englishman, invents a process that allows photographs to be copied.

1895 The Lumière brothers of France patent their original camera/projector using celluloid film with sprocket holes at the edge.

1948 American inventor Edwin Land develops the first instant camera, which is marketed by the Polaroid Corporation.

1956 A camera that records onto reel-to-reel magnetic videotape, rather than plastic film, is invented.

1980s First digital cameras prototyped.

1986 Disposable camera launched.

1992 The jpeg, a compressed file format for storing digital images, is introduced.

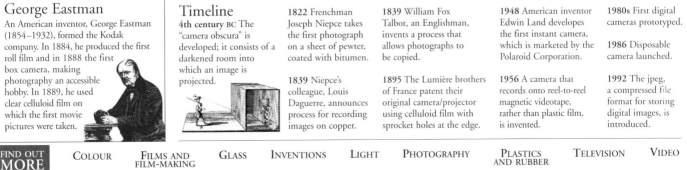

FIND OUT MORE   COLOUR   FILMS AND FILM-MAKING   GLASS   INVENTIONS   LIGHT   PHOTOGRAPHY   PLASTICS AND RUBBER   TELEVISION   VIDEO

Stills cameras

Early cameras

Image projected upside down

Fox Talbot's camera of 1835 required exposure times of over an hour.

Daguerreotype camera of mid-1800s was the first model sold to the public.

Shutter operated by a cord

Kodak Autographic Special of 1918 was an early roll-film camera.

Ensign of the 1930s, with a side viewfinder: was popular in sports photography.

Box made camera sturdy

Brownie Hawkeye of the 1940s reflected the new use of plastic in design.

Upper lens is for viewing

1950s Duaflex was modelled on the superior twin-lens cameras of the time.

35mm cameras

Shutter and film speed dial

Manual SLR camera needs to be focused and wound on manually.

Shutter release button

Automatic SLR camera has an automatic film-loading and wind-on mechanism.

Basic compact camera has a fixed length lens and built-in flash.

Zoom controlled by motor

Advanced compacts are often fitted with a zoom lens, giving extra flexibility.

Leica cameras were the first to use the small-format, 35mm film.

Image is seen here

Waist-level viewer attachment allows photos to be taken from waist height.

Medium- and large-format cameras

6 x 4.5 cm camera is a small, light, medium-format camera.

6 x 6 cm camera produces a square image and is used by many professionals.

Direct vision camera has rangefinder focusing lenses, reducing size and weight.

6 x 7 cm camera produces a rectangular image ideal for landscape photography.

6 x 9 cm camera produces large images that make very clear enlargements.

Large-format camera uses individual sheets of film for each image.

Special cameras

Large viewfinder

Underwater camera has large easy-to-read dials for use deep underwater.

Panoramic camera rotates to take a view of up to 360° in one exposure.

Moving bellows along track alters magnification

Bellows camera allows for a very wide range of image magnifications.

Film exit slot

Polaroid camera produces a finished photo seconds after taking the picture.

Built in flash

Disposable camera is simple and light, and is used only once.

Digital camera does not use film, but stores pictures digitally.

Movie cameras

Debro pavro was an early movie camera. The handle was turned to start filming.

Marey's rifle is a camera shaped like a rifle, with the lens in the barrel.

Magazines hold three strips of film separately

Technicolor three-strip camera produces good, but expensive films.

Cine 8 takes still photographs in rapid succession.

Images are recorded directly on video tape

Camcorders are hand-held video cameras, used by many individuals.

Trigger works like a shutter release

Matt-box keeps stray light out of the lens

CAMOUFLAGE AND COLOUR

ANIMALS HAVE EVOLVED different colours, shapes, and patterns that help them survive. Some, such as birds-of-paradise, are brightly coloured to attract a mate; others, such as the fire salamander, use colour to advertise that they are poisonous to eat. Animals, such as lapwings and polar bears, are camouflaged – coloured or patterned – in such a way that they blend with their surroundings. Camouflage helps animals to hide from predators, but it can also help predators to creep up on their prey.

Types of coloration

Coloration falls into two main categories: cryptic and phaneric. Cryptic colours and patterns help an animal to remain concealed, thus helping protect it from enemies, or assisting in the capture of its prey. The factors that cryptic species suppress – colour, movement, and relief – are exaggerated in phaneric species. Phaneric coloration makes an animal stand out. It can include the conspicuous display of brilliant colours, shapes, and actions, as demonstrated by birds-of-paradise.

Bright colours of male make him stand out and attract females.

Red-headed gouldian finch

Cryptic coloration

Cryptic coloration is common among birds. The plumage of many desert species blends perfectly with the ground colour of their habitat. Birds of the forest canopy, such as parrots, are frequently green to match the dense foliage in which they live. Not all members of the same species are of cryptic colours. Sometimes the female or nestlings, which are generally in greater need of concealment, may be of cryptic colour, while the male is conspicuously coloured to attract a mate.

Newly hatched lapwings match colour of straw.

Young lapwings in nest

Phaneric coloration

Phaneric coloration used by animals such as macaws and mandrills makes them stand out and be noticed. It is used between male and female in courtship displays, between parent and young and members of a group for purposes of recognition, between rival males in threat displays, and between predators and prey as warning signals, bluff, or to deflect attack. Long ear- and head-plumes, fans, elongated tail feathers, wattles, and inflatable air sacs are all used to attract attention.

Camouflage

For concealment to be effective, the colour and pattern of an animal's coat or skin must relate closely to its background. A bird's colour often harmonizes with its nesting requirements; some ground-nesting birds choose a nest site with surroundings of similar colour to their eggs as an aid to concealment. Colour and posture can be a highly effective form of camouflage. The many types of concealment include disruptive coloration, disguise, and immobility.

Disruptive coloration

Irregular patches of contrasting colours and tones of an animal's coat divert attention away from the shape of the animal, making it harder to recognize. Tigers and giraffes show disruptive coloration.

Tiger camouflaged in long grass

Giant spiny stick insect

Disguise

Cryptic coloration aims to disguise rather than conceal. The combination of colour, form, and posture can produce an almost exact replica of a commonplace object associated with the habitat. Stick insects, for example, resemble small twigs, while nightjars, when lying down, look like stones or wood fragments.

Mimicry

Mimicry is an extreme form of concealment. It occurs when a relatively defenceless or edible species looks like an aggressive or dangerous species. The mimic not only takes on the appearance of the object it is mimicking, but also adopts its behaviour, assuming characteristics that are completely alien to it. For example, harmless milk snakes resemble poisonous coral snakes so that other animals will not attack them. The monarch, a poisonous butterfly, is mimicked by a non-poisonous species, *Hypolimnus*, which is indistinguishable from it.

Coral snake

Milk snake

Milk snakes have stripes of the same colour as coral snakes, but in a different order.

Immobility

Effective camouflage is possible only if an animal remains still. Many animals react to danger by freezing. For example, if confronted with danger, reedbuck crouch down with their necks outstretched, and by remaining motionless, become hard to distinguish from their surroundings. Some birds, particularly ground-nesting birds such as nightjars, squat down to reduce the shadow they make.

Reedbuck

Assassin bug

Many species of assassin bugs resemble the insects on which they feed. This enables them to get close to their prey without being detected, before seizing it and injecting a toxic fluid. One species of assassin bug, *Salyavata variegata*, lives in termite nests. It camouflages itself by covering its body in debris, including the bodies of termites, and then enters the nest, unnoticed, to feed on the inhabitants.

Assassin bug covered in debris by termites' nest

Termite

Social displays

Social displays take many different forms, from threat display to courtship and bonding. Both cuttlefish and octopuses can change colour; they darken and flash different colours to intimidate rivals or enemies. The male Uganda kob, a type of antelope, establishes territorial breeding grounds by displaying along the boundary of his territory. Lowering his head, he makes a mock attack with his horns. This warns rival males to keep out of his territory, while at the same time, induces other females to join his harem.

Ring-tailed lemurs signalling with raised tails

Signalling

Signs and signals help animals to maintain contact, preserve the social hierarchy, and intimidate rivals and enemies. The signals have to be conspicuous and unmistakable. The ring-tailed lemurs of Madagascar raise their long black and white tails to waft scent at their rivals, and to enable all members of a group to maintain contact. The black rings encircling the cheetah's white-tipped tail enable the cubs to follow their parent, which would otherwise be invisible in the long grass. The young of ringed plovers have a white neck-band which helps the parents keep the brood together.

Strong feathers at the rear, attached to muscles, are used to raise the long feathers.

Peacock with tail feathers raised

Courtship

Many animals use courtship displays to attract a mate. The fiddler crab, for example, waves its outsize claw, the elephant seal inflates its nose, and the grouse spreads its tail and inflates its air sacs. Among the most impressive courtship displays are that of the male peacock, which spreads his brilliantly coloured tail plumage, and the elaborate rituals of birds-of-paradise and bowerbirds. These involve vibrating the body, fanning feathers, puffing out plumage, decorating nesting areas, and calling loudly.

Tail feathers overlap and rest on the ground when relaxed.

Peacock

Peacock starting to erect tail plumage.

Male calls as he starts to display.

Henry Walter Bates

The English naturalist and explorer, Henry Bates (1825–92) spent 11 years exploring the Amazon, returning with 8,000 species of previously unknown insects. In 1861, he published a paper on mimicry which made an important contribution to the theory of natural selection. He suggested that some harmless insects looked like harmful ones to discourage predators from attacking them.

Red and black froghopper

Warning signals

Animals use many methods to frighten off other animals. Warning colours make prey appear unpalatable to discourage predators. Many poisonous and venomous animals do not need to be camouflaged; they advertise themselves with bright coloured patterns of red, yellow, and black, which are recognized warning colours. Skunks' black and white coats warn they can squirt foul-smelling spray.

False warning

Many animals employ bluff as a means of defence. In birds, this may take the form of fluffing up feathers, spreading wings, and clacking beaks. Many frogs and toads blow themselves up, to appear larger; the hawkmoth caterpillar looks like a snake to intimidate enemies; and the Australian frilled lizard erects its frill and hisses to intimidate intruders.

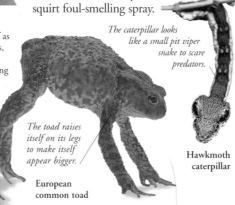

The caterpillar looks like a small pit viper snake to scare predators.

The toad raises itself on its legs to make itself appear bigger.

European common toad

Hawkmoth caterpillar

Seasonal change

Some Arctic animals, such as the polar bear and snowy owl, remain white throughout the year; others undergo a seasonal change. In far-northern latitudes, the stoat becomes completely white in winter, except for the tip of its tail, which remains black. In the warmer parts of its habitat, it can retain its russet coloration, become part-coloured, or change to white as needed. This ability to change colour provides the stoat with effective camouflage throughout the year.

Stoat with dark summer coat

Stoat with pale winter coat

FIND OUT MORE   BIRDS   BUGS   DEER AND ANTELOPES   FROGS AND TOADS   LIONS AND OTHER WILD CATS   MONKEYS AND OTHER PRIMATES   OWLS AND NIGHTJARS   POISONOUS ANIMALS   SNAKES

CAMPING AND HIKING

ONE OF THE MOST popular types of holiday, camping offers people the chance to enjoy the great outdoors at close quarters. For many people, their first experience of camping is as children, setting up a tent in their own back yard. But it is also a popular activity with adults who enjoy getting away from cities to explore the countryside, and perhaps even learning survival skills in the wild. Camping offers the freedom to choose to stay at one campsite throughout a holiday, or to set up camp at a different site each night. Whatever the type of holiday, it is important to take the appropriate clothing, food, and equipment.

An ideal campsite

Prevailing winds

Trees provide shelter from the wind.

River is a source of water for drinking and washing.

Ground is level and there is no danger of flooding.

Choosing a campsite

Many campers stay on organized campsites with shared cooking and washing facilities. Those who prefer to camp "in the wild" look for high, level, dry ground on which to pitch a tent. The best campsites are sheltered from the wind, and not too close to any rivers or dams.

Fire ingredients

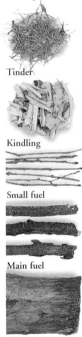

Tinder

Kindling

Small fuel

Main fuel

Large fuel

Making a teepee fire

Fires provide warmth and a means of cooking, but they can also be dangerous. Campers must make certain that a fire is permitted, safe, and will not harm their tent or the surroundings. They are especially careful if a strong wind is blowing.

1 The camper gathers the fuel he or she needs (ranging in size from twigs to branches), cuts out a square of turf, and puts a layer of sticks in the hole.

Make sure the fuel is dry.

2 The camper balances four sticks to meet at the top in a teepee shape, making sure the teepee has enough space for tinder inside the sticks.

3 Gradually, the camper adds more sticks, making the teepee as sturdy as possible, and puts some tinder, such as leaves and dry grass, inside.

Hole for putting in tinder

4 The camper lights the tinder with a match and gradually add more tinder, then twigs and larger pieces of fuel. He or she takes care not to knock the teepee over. When the teepee burns, it will collapse and create embers that can be used for cooking.

Keep a torch at the head of a sleeping bag.

Unpack things only as needed

The head of a sleeping bag should face the door.

Living in a tent

There is very little room inside a tent, so campers need to be well organized, otherwise they may be uncomfortable and lose things. To stop damp seeping in from the soil under a sleeping bag, campers put a waterproof sheet on the ground beneath the tent.

Things to take camping

It is better to take only the basic items of equipment camping. These include all the tools needed to set up a camp, as well as cooking and eating utensils. In addition, campers should take hard-wearing clothes to protect them against all types of weather.

Binoculars

Survival kit

First aid kit

Matches

Torch

Swiss army knife

Sewing kit

Wash kit, for example, soap and shampoo

Lip salve

Plastic Mug

Compass

Plastic plate and bowl

Cutlery

Food and water

For healthy eating, campers aim to maintain a balanced diet, including fruit and vegetables, bread, and food containing protein, such as fish and meat. If it is difficult or impossible for campers to buy food while they are away, they take tinned or freeze-dried foods, which will not perish. Campers should only drink water from approved sources. If necessary, they take water purifiers or a portable water filter.

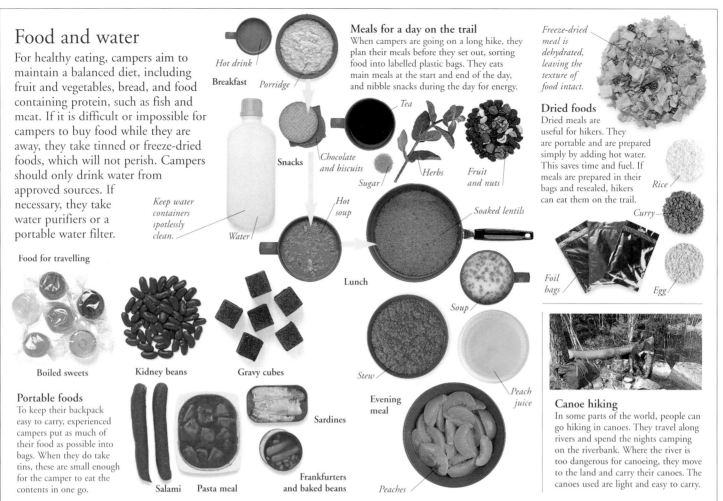

Hot drink

Breakfast *Porridge*

Keep water containers spotlessly clean.

Water

Snacks

Chocolate and biscuits

Sugar

Tea

Herbs

Fruit and nuts

Hot soup

Soaked lentils

Lunch

Soup

Stew

Evening meal

Peach juice

Peaches

Meals for a day on the trail
When campers are going on a long hike, they plan their meals before they set out, sorting food into labelled plastic bags. They eats main meals at the start and end of the day, and nibble snacks during the day for energy.

Freeze-dried meal is dehydrated, leaving the texture of food intact.

Dried foods
Dried meals are useful for hikers. They are portable and are prepared simply by adding hot water. This saves time and fuel. If meals are prepared in their bags and resealed, hikers can eat them on the trail.

Rice

Curry

Foil bags

Egg

Food for travelling

Boiled sweets

Kidney beans

Gravy cubes

Portable foods
To keep their backpack easy to carry, experienced campers put as much of their food as possible into bags. When they do take tins, these are small enough for the camper to eat the contents in one go.

Salami   *Pasta meal*

Sardines

Frankfurters and baked beans

Canoe hiking
In some parts of the world, people can go hiking in canoes. They travel along rivers and spend the nights camping on the riverbank. Where the river is too dangerous for canoeing, they move to the land and carry their canoes. The canoes used are light and easy to carry.

Caravanning

A popular alternative to camping is caravanning. Caravans are small, compact homes on wheels, which can be towed by a car to a campsite. They are more comfortable to live in than tents. Most have stoves, beds, and toilets, and some may even have refrigerators and showers. Some campsites have permanent, fixed caravans that you can rent for a holiday if you do not have your own.

Using a compass
Hikers take a map and a compass when they go on a long walk, so that they can follow the route and not get lost. A protractor compass, shown here, is popular because it is light, reliable, and accurate.

Hiking

Walking through the countryside, for a few hours or for up to several weeks, is a form of exercise enjoyed by people of all ages. Hikers walk in groups, so that if an accident occurs, at least two can go for help together, and one can stay with the injured member of the party. Hikers should be fully equipped for the sort of journey they are making and should tell someone where they are going.

Shoulder straps can be adjusted to fit.

Ice pick

Windproof jacket with a hood.

Ice hammer

Backpacking
A comfortable way to carry belongings, backpacks range from light day packs to large packs that have space for everything needed for several days' hiking. They sit as high as possible on the shoulders, to distribute weight.

Mountain walking
The most difficult and dangerous form of hiking is mountain climbing. Mountain climbers enjoy testing their strength and skill on steep rock faces. They need to be particularly fit, and use special climbing equipment.

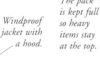

Crampon

Tent poles and pegs in the same bag

The pack is kept full so heavy items stay at the top.

Sleeping bag at the bottom.

How to pack a backpack
To keep the contents of a backpack dry, line it with a plastic bag and put everything in separate plastic bags. Pack the lighter, bulkier things at the bottom and the heavier things at the top. Spare clothes can be packed down the back to protect the spine.

FIND OUT MORE   ENERGY   EXPLORATION   FIRE   FIRST AID   FOOD   HEALTH AND FITNESS

C

CANADA

THE WORLD'S SECOND LARGEST country, Canada covers the northern part of the North American continent and is made up of ten provinces and three territories. Canada borders Alaska and the Pacific Ocean to the west, and the Atlantic Ocean to the east. Winters in the northern third of the country, much of which lies within the Arctic Circle, are so severe that very few people can live there. About 80 per cent of Canadians live within 320 km (200 miles) of the US border. Canada has huge forests, rich mineral resources, and open, fertile farmland.

C

Ottawa

Canada's capital sits on the south bank of the Ottawa River, and has a population of 921,000. The city has clean, wide streets, many lined with parks. The Rideau Canal, part of a complex of lakes and canals linking Ottawa with Lake Ontario, freezes in winter, becoming the world's longest skating rink.

Skating on the Rideau Canal

Physical features

Covered in lakes, rivers, and forests, Canada has one-third of the world's fresh water. Frozen islands lie in the Arctic, high mountains in the west, and vast prairies in the south.

45°C (113°F)   -63°C (-81°F)

21°C (70°F)   -11°C (12°F)

871 mm (34 in)

Climate

Most of Canada has a continental climate with long, bitterly cold winters and hot, humid summers. Coastal areas are generally mild, especially the Pacific west coast. The glaciers and ice-caps of the north are permanently frozen.

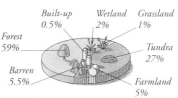

Built-up 0.5%   Wetland 2%   Grassland 1%

Forest 59%   Tundra 27%

Barren 5.5%   Farmland 5%

Land use

Canada's vast prairies are used for growing wheat. The forests support a thriving timber industry. Only five per cent of Canada's land area is cultivated.

Rocky Mountains

The snow-capped Rocky Mountains dominate western Canada, extending south into the USA. Canada's highest mountain is Logan, at 5,959 m (19,551 ft).

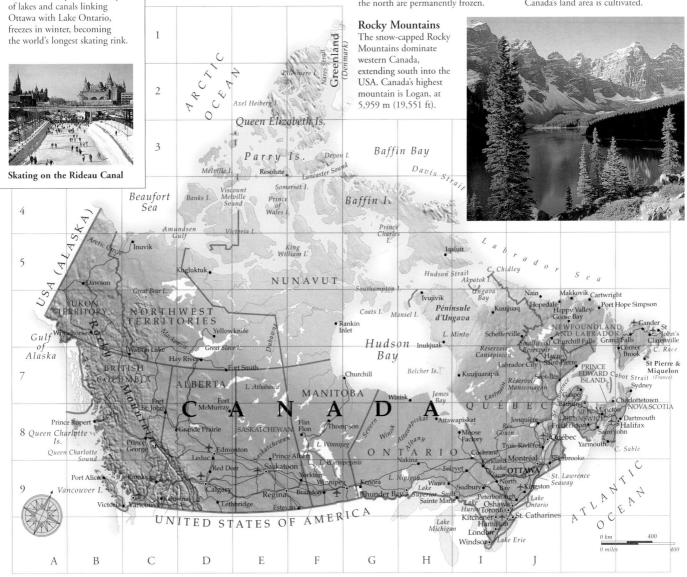

People

Most Canadians have European ancestors who emigrated to Canada from the UK, France, Germany, Scandinavia, and Italy. There are large numbers of Ukrainians, Indians, and Chinese. The indigenous peoples of Canada form about four per cent.

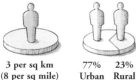

3 per sq km (8 per sq mile)

77% Urban **23% Rural**

Inuit
The Inuit are one of the country's indigenous groups, and almost 50,000 Inuits live in northern Canada. One-quarter are settled on Baffin Island, in the east Arctic, and speak their own language, *Inuktitut*. In 1999 the Inuit homeland of Nunavut was made a territory.

Leisure

Many Canadians enjoy outdoor activities. In the summer, people sail, raft, canoe, or simply enjoy one of Canada's many well-kept parks. The major spectator sports are hockey, baseball, and football.

Winter sports
Plentiful snow makes skiing and ice-skating popular with many Canadians. Ice hockey is played everywhere, from frozen backyards to national stadiums. Calgary hosted the 1988 Winter Olympics.

Hardwood stick

Calgary Stampede
One of the world's largest rodeos, the Calgary Stampede attracts one million visitors every year. Held in July, the 10-day rodeo is an exciting recreation of the Wild West. People dress up in cowboy outfits and try their luck at calf roping, chuck wagon racing, and bronco riding.

Tough rubber puck is hit into the goal.

Farming

Five per cent of Canada's land is arable, and the country is a top exporter of wheat, oats, maize, and barley. Forest products and fish are also key exports. Cattle and pigs are raised on the pastures of the southeast. Three per cent of the work-force are farmers.

Apple

Cranberries

Niagara Fruit Belt
The land between Lakes Ontario and Erie is called the "Niagara Fruit Belt" because the soil and climate are ideal for growing soft fruit, such as cherries and peaches. Apples and cranberries flourish in British Columbia. In the east, the maple tree, whose leaf is Canada's national emblem, yields rich syrup, a favourite served with sweet pancakes.

Maple leaves

Wheat
Canada's main cereal crop is wheat, and on the eastern prairies, around Saskatchewan, wheat farming is a way of life. About half of the 29,870,000 tonnes (32,930,000 tons) grown every year are exported.

Transport

The 8,000-km (5,000-mile) Trans-Canada Highway links the east and west coasts. The St Lawrence Seaway provides trade links for the eastern provinces. A vast air network, railways, rivers, and the lakes are also used for transport.

St Lawrence Seaway
Opened in 1959, the St Lawrence Seaway links the Great Lakes with the St Lawrence River and the Atlantic. Over 725 km (450 miles), a series of locks enables ocean-going ships, from all over the world, to sail inland.

Snowplough
Canada's long, cold winters bring heavy snow and ice to the country, making travelling by road difficult and dangerous. Snowploughs work through the day and night to keep roads clear. Most Canadian roads are wide to allow room for snow to be piled up on either side.

Industry

The centre of Canada's industry is at the western end of Lake Ontario, a region known as "the Golden Horseshoe". Canadian factories process foods, assemble cars, and make steel, chemical products, and paper. The service industries are thriving, and tourism now employs one in ten Canadians.

Nickel

Zinc

Mining
Minerals have been one of the major factors in the growth of Canada's economy. The country is the world's largest producer of zinc ore and uranium, and second of nickel and asbestos.

Forestry
Canada's abundant forests have made it the world's second largest exporter of softwood (fir and pine) and wood pulp. Ten per cent of Canada's labour force work in the lumber industry, where timber is used as a raw material. British Columbia, Québec, and Ontario are the major timber-producing provinces.

Québec
At the heart of French Canada, Québec City has many stone houses and 17th-century buildings, and its old town was declared a World Heritage Site in 1985. The province of Québec is home to nearly 7,500,000 people. More than three-quarters of the people are of French descent, and keep the French language and culture alive. There have been many attempts by the province to claim independence from Canada.

Château Frontenac, Québec old town

FIND OUT MORE | CANADA, HISTORY OF | FARMING | FISHING INDUSTRY | FORESTS | LAKES | NATIVE AMERICANS | PORTS AND WATERWAYS | ROCKS AND MINERALS | TUNDRA | WINTER SPORTS

CANADA, HISTORY OF

FOR MOST OF ITS history, Canada has been home to Native Americans and Inuits. They were descendants of the first people to settle there during the Ice Age, and built advanced cultures based on hunting and trapping fish and animals. In 1497, the first Europeans visited the country, establishing settlements in the early 1600s. In the 18th century, French and British armies fought for control of the entire country. The British won, but a sizeable French community has remained in Québec to this day.

First Canadians
The first inhabitants of Canada were peoples from northern Asia who crossed a land bridge from Siberia and moved south through America more than 20,000 years ago. The Inuits lived in the Arctic regions, while other Native American peoples occupied the plains and coastal areas. They all developed their own distinctive cultures. For example, the tribes of the northwest coast recorded their family history on totem poles, carving out representations of the family spirits on the trunks of cedar trees.

Jacques Cartier
The French sea captain Jacques Cartier (1491–1557) was hired by Francis I of France, to look for a northwest passage to China round the north of America. In 1534, he sailed into the Gulf of St Lawrence, and, in 1535, discovered the St Lawrence River. As he sailed up the river, he stopped at two Indian villages – Stadacona (modern Québec) and Hochelaga (Montreal). As a result, French immigrants began to settle by the St Lawrence River.

Fur trading
European settlers were attracted to Canada by the wealth to be made from furs and skins of animals trapped in the forests. The English-owned Hudson's Bay Company, established in 1670, and other trading companies set up fortified trading posts to trade furs and other goods with local Indian tribes. Québec (established 1608) and Montreal (1642) became important centres of the fur trade.

Traders travelled by canoe in order to reach the trading post.

Missionaries built churches to convert Native Americans.

Wigwams made of birch wood covered with skins or bark.

Houses and walls were built of wood from the forests.

Trading post

Capture of Québec
In 1759, British forces led by General James Wolfe attacked Québec, capital of the French colony of New France. Wolfe captured the city arriving from the Gulf of St. Lawrence with a flotilla of 168 ships that carried over 30,000 men. However, both he and the French commander, Louis, Marquis de Montcalm, were killed. All of French North America came under British control.

Wolfe's flotilla arrives in Québec.

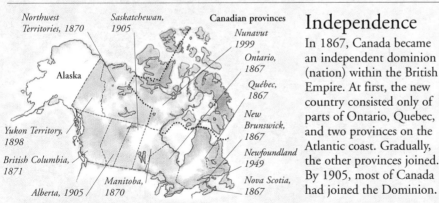

Northwest Territories, 1870
Saskatchewan, 1905
Canadian provinces
Nunavut 1999
Ontario, 1867
Québec, 1867
Alaska
New Brunswick, 1867
Newfoundland 1949
Yukon Territory, 1898
British Columbia, 1871
Manitoba, 1870
Alberta, 1905
Nova Scotia, 1867

Independence
In 1867, Canada became an independent dominion (nation) within the British Empire. At first, the new country consisted only of parts of Ontario, Quebec, and two provinces on the Atlantic coast. Gradually, the other provinces joined. By 1905, most of Canada had joined the Dominion.

Immigration
At the end of the 19th century, Canada's economy expanded and two transcontinental railways improved communications. Canada became an attractive place for European emigrants, and between 1891 and 1914, over three million people came to Canada in search of work and a new life. Canada's government encouraged Europeans to emigrate, promising future citizens health and wealth in their new home.

Canadian government poster

Timeline
1497 John Cabot, an Italian sailor, claims Newfoundland for Britain.

1534–35 Jacques Cartier explores the Gulf of St. Lawrence for France; then discovers the St. Lawrence River.

1605 French establish the first European colony at Port Royal, Nova Scotia.

1754 French and Indian War between Britain and France. France forced to relinquish Québec to Britain.

1846 Oregon Treaty confirms present borders with USA

1949 Founder member of NATO

1968 Québec Party formed to demand independence for Québec.

1989 UK transfers all power relating to Canada in British law.

1998 Government apologises to Native Americans over land.

Canadian flag

Québec
Canada recognized both its English- and French-speakers as equal, but in the 1960s, many people in French-speaking Québec began to press for their province to become independent. In 1982, Québec was given the status of a "distinct society", but referendums seeking independence were defeated in 1980 and 1995.

FIND OUT MORE
EXPLORATION | FRANCE, HISTORY OF | NATIVE AMERICANS | NORTH AMERICA, HISTORY OF | UNITED KINGDOM, HISTORY OF | UNITED STATES, HISTORY OF

CARIBBEAN

HUNDREDS OF ISLANDS lie in the Caribbean Sea, east of the USA and Central America, and stretching west into the Atlantic Ocean. These Caribbean islands, also known as the West Indies, take their name from the Caribs, the original inhabitants of the region, until the Spanish arrived in 1492. Most islanders today are descendents of African slaves brought to work in plantations between the 16th and 19th centuries. The islands have a tropical climate, turquoise waters, and fine beaches, and have developed a booming tourist industry. However, many people are poor and live by farming.

Volcanic islands
Many Caribbean islands are made of volcanic rocks that emerged from the ocean millions of years ago. Some, such as the St Lucian Gros Piton, 798 m (2,619 ft), and the Petit Piton, 750 m (2,461 ft), are the remains of ancient volcanoes that rise up from the sea on the west coast, near the town of Soufrière. One or two are still active, such as La Soufrière, at 1,219 m (4,000 ft) on St Vincent.

Physical features

Long, sandy beaches, tropical seas, and fine natural harbours have earned the Caribbean islands a reputation for beauty. Most of the islands are forested and mountainous. Some are volcanic in origin, others are founded on coral reefs. Hurricanes, earthquakes, and active volcanoes shake parts of the region from time to time.

Coral islands
The warm, tropical seas of the Caribbean provide ideal conditions for corals. Some of the Caribbean's volcanic islands, such as Barbados and the Cayman Islands, are fringed with coral reefs, which protect them against the lashing waves. The 700 islands and 2,300 islets of the Bahamas are entirely built up of coral, which can be viewed from the bridge that links Nassau with Paradise Island.

Hurricanes
Powerful tropical storms called hurricanes sweep the Caribbean between May and October every year, often causing great damage and economic hardship. They begin as thunderstorms that are whipped up by high winds and warm waters to form destructive stormclouds, swirling around a single centre at up to 360 kmh (220 mph). The violent winds and torrential rain can last for 18 hours.

Regional climate
The countries of the Caribbean all enjoy a warm, tropical climate. Mountainous islands, such as the Windwards, receive three times as much rainfall as lower areas. Most islands have a wet, hurricane-prone season between June and November. From January to March, it is generally dry and pleasant.

28°C (82°F) 23°C (73°F)

1,167 mm (46 in)

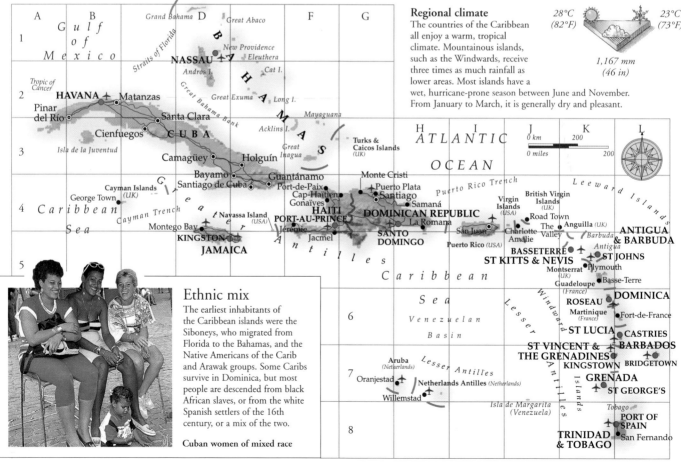

Ethnic mix
The earliest inhabitants of the Caribbean islands were the Siboneys, who migrated from Florida to the Bahamas, and the Native Americans of the Carib and Arawak groups. Some Caribs survive in Dominica, but most people are descended from black African slaves, or from the white Spanish settlers of the 16th century, or a mix of the two.

Cuban women of mixed race

Cuba

The largest island in the Caribbean, Cuba has fertile lowlands set between three large mountainous regions. Sugar, rice, tobacco, and coffee are grown on the lowlands, and chromium and nickel are mined. Formerly a Spanish colony, Cuba has been a communist state since 1959. Hostile politics caused the USA to impose a trade embargo, which has disabled Cuba's economy and kept it agricultural.

Sugar is extracted from the cane.

Sugar
With an annual production of 50,000,000 tonnes (55,000,000 tons), sugar-cane is Cuba's largest crop. It is grown around Havana and processed in the city's factories. Cuba is one of the world's largest producers but suffered a decline in the 1990s following the collapse of one of its main customers, the Soviet Union.

Communism
The only communist state in the Caribbean, Cuba is led by Fidel Castro (b. 1926), who led the revolution in 1959. Under Castro, and with Soviet help, Cuba made considerable social and economic progress, although living standards suffered with the breakup of Soviet communism in 1991. US policies remain hostile.

Havana
Situated in a natural harbour, Cuba's chief port and capital, Havana, was founded by the Spanish in 1515. Its old town has many ancient buildings and cobbled streets. There are no shanty towns here, unlike many capitals in the region, but of its 2,328,000 people, half live in sub-standard houses.

Cigars
Cuba's fertile soil and warm climate are ideal for growing high-quality tobacco. Havana cigars are popular all over the world and are made from a blend of at least five different types of tobacco. Cigars are still rolled by hand at long wooden tables.

CUBA FACTS
CAPITAL CITY	Havana
AREA	110,860 sq km (42,803 sq miles)
POPULATION	11,200,000
MAIN LANGUAGE	Spanish
MAJOR RELIGION	Christian
CURRENCY	Cuban Peso

Bahamas

Located to the northeast of Cuba, the Bahamas extend south for about 965 km (600 miles). Of the 3,000 coral islands and islets, only 30 are inhabited. Most of the people are black, but on Spanish Wells island, there are around 1,200 white descendants of Puritan settlers. Tourism, fishing, and financial services flourish on the islands.

Festival
Music and dancing are everywhere in the Caribbean, but especially so at the Junkanoo Festival on the Bahamas islands. Held at the end of every year, Junkanoo is a lively celebration with street dancing, music, and colourful parades where people wear wild costumes and blow whistles. The festival has roots in the celebrations of a slave leader called John Canoe, and slaves' days off at Christmas.

BAHAMAS FACTS
CAPITAL CITY	Nassau
AREA	13,940 sq km (5,382 sq miles)
POPULATION	308,000
MAIN LANGUAGE	English
MAJOR RELIGION	Christian
CURRENCY	Bahamian dollar

Jamaica

The third largest island of the Caribbean, Jamaica is a land of springs, rivers, waterfalls, and sandy beaches. A few wealthy families dominate the island, but the slum areas around Kingston are controlled by violent gangs. Many of the people of those areas are Rastafarians, worshippers of the former Emperor of Ethiopia. Jamaica is a prosperous country, with booming tourist, mining, and farming industries. Cricket is a popular game.

Reggae
Jamaica's distinctive form of popular music, reggae, began in the 1960s as an offshoot of rhythm and blues, with songs calling for social and political change. Bob Marley (1945–81), whose band won world fame in the 1970s, is a reggae icon, and his birthday is celebrated by all Jamaicans.

Women
The Caribbean women's rights movement began in Jamaica, and many Jamaican women hold senior posts in economic and political life. An increasing number of women prefer to be single mothers, especially those who have careers. Women also dominate the growing data-processing industry, largely because they work for lower wages than men.

Okra (Lady's fingers)

Breadfruit

Dasheen, or taro

Vegetables
Jamaicans grow a wide range of vegetables. *Dasheen*, or *taro*, is a staple vegetable whose root and leaves are eaten. There are more than 1,000 varieties of *dasheen*, and it is also used for medicinal purposes. Okra, or lady's fingers, are green pods that are used in "pepperpot stews". Breadfruit, with a creamy, pulpy texture, grow to 13 cm (5 in) wide, and are eaten baked or roasted.

Bauxite
Jamaica is the world's third largest producer of bauxite, the ore from which aluminium is made. Refineries produce alumina, the next stage in producing the metal, worth ten times as much as the ore. This provides about half of Jamaica's export income, and accounts for 10 per cent of global output.

JAMAICA FACTS
CAPITAL CITY	Kingston
AREA	10,990 sq km (4,243 sq miles)
POPULATION	2,600,000
MAIN LANGUAGE	English
MAJOR RELIGIONS	Christian, Rastafarian
CURRENCY	Jamaican dollar

C

Haiti

Occupying the western third of the island of Hispaniola, Haiti is one of the most mountainous countries in the Caribbean. It is also the poorest. About 95 per cent of its people are descendents of black slaves. The country is overcrowded, and has suffered deforestation, soil erosion, and desertification, as well as a turbulent political history.

Port-au-Prince
Smart modern hotels have lured many visitors to Haiti's capital, Port-au-Prince. The city has two cathedrals, a university, and many government buildings. However, it also has the worst slums in the Caribbean, most of which are found to the north of the centre. They have no water facilities and are overcrowded.

Voodoo
A Haitian blend of West African religions and Christianity, voodoo uses drums, singing, and dance. Its followers believe that through worship of spirits, they can live in harmony with nature and their dead. Many celebrations coincide with Christmas and the Mexican Day of the Dead.

Voodooists on Gede, or All Saint's Day

HAITI FACTS

CAPITAL CITY Port-au-Prince

AREA 27,750 sq km (10,714 sq miles)

POPULATION 8,300,000

MAIN LANGUAGES French, French Creole

MAJOR RELIGIONS Christian, Voodoo

CURRENCY Gourde

Puerto Rico

About 1,600 km (994 miles) southeast of Miami, the crowded island of Puerto Rico is a self-governing territory of the USA. It is home to more than 3.8 million people, of African and Spanish descent, of whom half live in the capital, San Juan. An old walled city, it has colonial buildings.

Balconies, old San Juan

Dominican Republic

Lying 966 km (600 miles) southeast of Florida, the Dominican Republic spreads across the eastern two-thirds of Hispaniola. It has the Caribbean's highest peak, Pico Duarte, 3,175 m (10,417 ft), and also its lowest point, crocodile-infested Lake Enriquillo, 44 m (144 ft) below sea-level. Nickel, amber, and gold mining are important industries, and holidaymakers flock to the island for its long, pearly beaches, modern hotels, and wildlife.

People
With a higher standard of living than neighbouring Haiti, the Dominican Republic provides good healthcare for its people. The mixed race middle classes form about 73 per cent of the population. The minority of blacks work as farmers, selling their produce at market.

Farming
About 24 per cent of the labour force work on farms, which are mostly in the north and east of the country, and in the San Juan valley. Sugar, tobacco, and cocoa are main crops, and, although the market has slowed, most are exported to the USA.

Tobacco leaves are hung upside down to dry and then made into cigars and cigarettes.

DOMINICAN REPUBLIC FACTS

CAPITAL CITY Santo Domingo

AREA 48,380 sq km (18,679 sq miles)

POPULATION 8,500,000

MAIN LANGUAGES Spanish, French Creole

MAJOR RELIGION Christian

CURRENCY Dominican Republic peso

Tourism
The Dominican Republic is the largest tourist destination in the Caribbean, attracting two million each year. The industry brings in half of the country's earnings and provides much-needed jobs.

St Kitts and Nevis

The two islands of St Kitts (or St Christopher) and Nevis sit in the northern part of the Leeward Islands. Both are mountainous, and their idyllic, palm-fringed beaches attract many tourists. Most people are descendents of black Africans, and nearly all work in farming or tourism.

ST KITTS AND NEVIS FACTS

CAPITAL CITY Basseterre

AREA 261 sq km (101 sq miles)

POPULATION 41,000

MAIN LANGUAGE English

MAJOR RELIGION Christian

CURRENCY Eastern Caribbean dollar

Sugar-cane
The main crop on St Kitts is sugar-cane, which accounts for 25 per cent of exports and provides 12 per cent of jobs. Low world prices and hurricane damage have created problems.

Antigua and Barbuda

The largest of the Leeward Islands, Antigua has two dependencies: Barbuda, a small, coral island bursting with wildlife, and Redonda, an uninhabited rock with its own king. The blue lagoons and corals that surround Antigua teem with tropical fish.

ANTIGUA AND BARBUDA FACTS

CAPITAL CITY St John's

AREA 442 sq km (170 sq miles)

POPULATION 66,400

MAIN LANGUAGE English

MAJOR RELIGION Christian

CURRENCY Eastern Caribbean dollar

Yachting
The harbour at St John's has an annual Sailing Week that attracts many visitors and rich yachtspeople. Cruise ships and luxury boats call at the 18th-century Nelson's Dockyard.

C

Dominica

The largest and most mountainous of the Windward Islands, Dominica has some of the finest scenery in the Caribbean, with rainforests containing 200 wildlife species. Bananas and coconuts are principal exports; prawn farming is proving successful.

DOMINICA FACTS

CAPITAL CITY Roseau

AREA 754 sq km (291 sq miles)

POPULATION 73,000

MAIN LANGUAGES English, French

MAJOR RELIGION Christian

CURRENCY Eastern Caribbean dollar

Carib Reservation

In the 1900s, the British forced the Caribs to move to a reservation. Today, the Carib reservation, on the east coast of the island, is home to more than 2,000 Caribs, descendants of the original inhabitants. Within the reservation – a popular tourist attraction – Caribs follow traditional lifestyles although their language has died out. Many Carib craftspeople make a living selling bags made from banana leaves and grasses.

St Lucia

The beautiful island of St Lucia has clear seas, sandy beaches, and striking volcanic mountains. Most people work in farming, tourism, or industry. Each year, 150,000 tonnes (165,000 tons) of bananas are exported.

ST LUCIA FACTS

CAPITAL CITY Castries

AREA 620 sq km (239 sq miles)

POPULATION 156,300

MAIN LANGUAGE English

MAJOR RELIGION Christian

CURRENCY Eastern Caribbean dollar

Ecotourism

St Lucia's lush rainforests, boiling springs, and twin Piton peaks are attractions that lure visitors to the island. Aromatic tropical plants, trees, and flowers grow everywhere.

Barbados

Known as the "singular island", Barbados lies 160 km (100 miles) east of the Caribbean chain. Barbados retains a strong English influence, and many Britons retire to the island. The people of Barbados, called Bajans, enjoy some of the Caribbean's highest living standards.

BARBADOS FACTS

CAPITAL CITY Bridgetown

AREA 430 sq km (166 sq miles)

POPULATION 268,000

MAIN LANGUAGE English

MAJOR RELIGION Christian

CURRENCY Barbados dollar

Tourism

Barbados has one of the Caribbean's most well-developed and lucrative tourist industries. About 556,000 people visit the island every year.

St Vincent and the Grenadines

The quiet island of St Vincent is fertile and volcanic, while its 100 tiny sister islands of the Grenadines are flat coral reefs. Both are exclusive holiday resorts, and their waters are popular with yachtspeople. Bananas are the main export.

Arrowroot

St Vincent is the world's largest producer of arrowroot, a starchy liquid that is removed from the arrowroot plant. It is used as a thickening agent in foods, and more recently, as a fine finish for computer paper. Arrowroot is St Vincent's second largest export.

Arrowroot   Arrowroot powder

ST VINCENT AND THE GRENADINES FACTS

CAPITAL CITY Kingstown

AREA 389 sq km (151 sq miles)

POPULATION 115,500

MAIN LANGUAGE English

MAJOR RELIGION Christian

CURRENCY Eastern Caribbean dollar

Grenada

The most southerly of the Windwards, Grenada rises from a rugged coast to a high, forested interior. A former British colony, Grenada has built its economy on agriculture and tourism. Its people are of African or mixed origin.

Nutmeg

Ginger

Cinnamon

GRENADA FACTS

CAPITAL CITY St George's

AREA 340 sq km (131 sq miles)

POPULATION 98,000

MAIN LANGUAGE English

MAJOR RELIGION Christian

CURRENCY Eastern Caribbean dollar

Spices

Grenada is described as the "spice island". It grows about two-thirds of the world's nutmeg, and, with Indonesia, dominates the market. Large quantities of cloves, mace, cinnamon, ginger, bay leaves, saffron, and pepper are also cultivated on the island.

Trinidad and Tobago

The low-lying island of Trinidad and its smaller partner, Tobago, lie just off the coast of Venezuela. The islands have a vivid, cosmopolitan culture, home to people from every continent. Both have fertile farmland, fine beaches, and abundant wildlife.

Steel bands

Trinidad and Tobago are the home of steel bands, calypso, and limbo dancing. The first drums, or *pans*, began as empty oil containers. Today, drums are hand-decorated and tuned so that melodies can be played on them. They provide the beat for lively calypso songs.

TRINIDAD AND TOBAGO FACTS

CAPITAL CITY Port-of-Spain

AREA 5,128 sq km (1,980 sq miles)

POPULATION 1,300,000

MAIN LANGUAGE English

MAJOR RELIGIONS Christian, Hindu, Muslim

CURRENCY Trinidad and Tobago dollar

FIND OUT MORE   CARIBBEAN, HISTORY OF   CHRISTIANITY   FARMING   FESTIVALS   ISLANDS   MUSIC   RELIGIONS   ROCKS AND MINERALS   SLAVERY   VOLCANOES

CARIBBEAN, HISTORY OF

FOR CENTURIES, the Caribbean islands were home to the Carib and Arawak peoples. Their way of life was abruptly disturbed when Europeans arrived in the 1490s. Within 100 years, most had been wiped out by new European rulers who brought thousands of Africans into the Caribbean to work on sugar plantations. The sugar-based economy continued until its decline in the late 19th century. From the mid-1960s, the islands gradually gained independence from European control.

Original inhabitants
The Caribs were expert navigators, travelling great distances in wooden canoes. The Arawaks were skilled craftworkers, who produced baskets and furniture.

Arawak-style wooden seat from the Bahamas

Spanish conquest
The arrival of the Spanish-sponsored navigator Christopher Columbus in the Caribbean in 1492 transformed the region. Convoys of galleons laden with gold and other treasures from the Spanish empire in South America soon crossed the sea on their way back to Spain. Within a few years, Spanish armies had conquered and settled almost every island. Most of the Caribs were killed by the invaders.

Columbus's ship, the Santa Maria

European settlement
In the 16th century, with unofficial government backing, English, French, and Dutch pirates raided Spanish treasure ships. They also captured many of the smaller islands. Settlers from Europe arrived, and by 1750, most of the islands were under British, French, or Dutch rule.

— Route of trading ships

NORTH AMERICA

Crops taken to England

EUROPE

Manufactured goods taken to Africa

CARIBBEAN

AFRICA

Slaves taken to Caribbean

Toussaint L'Ouverture
Ex-slave Toussaint L'Ouverture (1743–1803) led a revolt of slaves in French-ruled Haiti in the 1790s. He declared the country a republic, but the French regained control and took him to France, where he died.

Rastafarians
Many Jamaicans are Rastafarians. They believe that the last emperor of Ethiopia, Ras Tafari, or Haile Selassie, was the new messiah who would lead his people back to Africa.

Plantations
Europeans set up plantations to satisfy demand for sugar and tobacco in Europe. African slaves worked on the plantations. By 1750, the Caribbean produced most of the world's sugar.

Sugar cane

Tobacco

Slave trade
Most of the Caribbean slave trade was controlled from English ports. Ships left England for West Africa with goods to barter for slaves. The slaves were shipped across the Atlantic. Sugar, tobacco, and other crops were then taken back to England for sale.

Cuban War
In 1895, following an earlier, unsuccessful uprising, the Cubans rose in revolt against their Spanish rulers. In 1898, the USA declared war on Spain, and freed Cuba.

Emigration
After World War II, many people left the Caribbean in search of work and a better standard of living in Europe. In 1948, the *Empire Windrush* took 492 emigrants from Kingston, Jamaica to London, UK. Over the next 20 years, thousands of Caribbean islanders emigrated to Britain.

Fidel Castro
In 1959, Fidel Castro (b.1927) became the President of Cuba and introduced many social reforms. The US government tried to depose him in 1961, and he turned to the USSR for help. When Soviet nuclear missiles were installed in Cuba in 1962, the world came close to nuclear war.

Timeline
1300s Caribs drive out Arawak people from the eastern Caribbean islands.

1492 Christopher Columbus lands in the Bahamas.

1500s The Spanish take control of the Caribbean.

1700s French, British, Dutch, and Danes capture many islands.

1804 Haiti becomes first Caribbean island to achieve independence from European rule.

1898–1902 Cuba under rule of USA.

1933 Fulgencio Batista becomes ruler of Cuba.

1948 *Empire Windrush* takes first emigrants to Britain.

Capturing a slave

1959 Cuban Revolution; Fidel Castro takes power.

1962 Cuban missile crisis brings the USA and the USSR to the brink of nuclear war.

1962 Jamaica becomes the first British Caribbean colony to win independence.

1962–83 Most British islands win independence; Dutch and French islands remain tied to Europeans.

1983 USA overthrows left-wing regime in Grenada.

Flag of Jamaica

1994 USA intervenes to secure democracy in Haiti, after years of dictatorship on the island.

FIND OUT MORE   AFRICA, EAST   COLUMBUS, CHRISTOPHER   EMPIRES   EXPLORATION   FRANCE, HISTORY OF   GOVERNMENTS AND POLITICS   SLAVERY   SPAIN, HISTORY OF

C

CARNIVOROUS PLANTS

PLANTS THAT catch and "eat" insects are called carnivorous plants. These plants fall into two groups. Some species, such as the Venus flytrap, have active traps with moving parts. Other species have passive traps, catching their victims on a sticky surface or drowning them in a pool of fluid. Carnivorous plants live in areas where the soil is poor in nitrates and other nutrients, such as bogs, peatlands, and swamps. They obtain extra nutrients by catching insects, which are digested by special juices.

Monkey-cup pitcher plant

Tendril

Pitcher plants from Southeast Asia form traps that hang from their leaves.

Hanging pitcher

Passive traps

The lid and the smooth rim are often brightly coloured to attract insects.

Most carnivorous plants have passive traps. Usually the leaves of these plants have evolved to catch insects in a variety of ways. Some are sticky, others form pit-fall traps with fluid at the bottom and are called pitcher plants.

Rim of the pitcher contains nectar.

The lid stays closed while the pitcher develops.

Mouth of pitcher

Insects fall into the liquid and are digested.

Development of a pitcher plant

1 A young leaf tip extends into a tendril.

2 An upturned swelling appears at the end.

3 The swelling develops into a pitcher.

4 The lid opens when the pitcher is mature.

American pitcher plants
Although they catch their prey in the same way as other pitcher plants, American pitcher plants grow up from the ground rather than hanging from leaves. The inside of the pitcher is slippery and lined with downward pointing hairs which prevent the insects from escaping. The liquid below drowns and slowly digests them.

Pitcher plant

Pitcher is made of leaves joined at the edges.

Butterworts
These small plants have sticky leaves. Small flies are attracted to their smell and get stuck. The leaves slowly roll up, and the insects are digested by juices that ooze out of the leaf.

Common butterwort

Leaf

Sundew flowers develop at the end of a long stalk.

A fly stuck to the hairs on a sundew leaf

Cape sundew

Active traps

Any trap with moving parts is called an active trap. These include plants such as sundews and butterworts, and the Venus flytrap.

Sundews
The upper surface of a sundew leaf is covered with red hairs that secrete drops of clear, sticky liquid. Insects get stuck, then the edges of the leaf slowly roll inward enclosing the insect, and the plant secretes juices that digest it.

Sticky leaf

Bladderworts
These are rootless water plants. Their leaves and stems bear tiny bladders with a lid covered in sensitive hairs. If a creature brushes the hairs, the lid of the bladder flips open. Water rushes in, carrying the victim with it.

Greater bladderwort

Venus flytrap
The most spectacular of all the carnivorous plants is the Venus flytrap. It is related to the sundews but has evolved a more elaborate trap. The Venus flytrap grows wild only in one small patch of marshy ground on the border of North and South Carolina, USA. Its trap springs closed when an insect touches the hairs on its surface.

Closed trap

Stimulation of at least three trigger hairs sets off the mechanism that closes the trap.

Surface of the trap

Venus flytrap

Magnified view of a trigger hair

How a Venus flytrap works

1 An insect lands on a leaf, touching the sensitive trigger hairs.

2 The leaf closes, and the spines interlock, trapping the insect.

3 The trap is fully closed in 30 minutes, and digestion begins.

Trigger hair

Trap is fringed with long spines.

Insect is trapped in one-fifth of a second.

FIND OUT MORE   ASIAN WILDLIFE   FLOWERS   INSECTS   NORTH AMERICAN WILDLIFE   PLANTS   PLANTS, ANATOMY   PLANTS, DEFENCE   PLANTS, REPRODUCTION   SOUTH AMERICAN WILDLIFE

CARS AND TRUCKS

OF ALL THE DIFFERENT FORMS of transport, cars have the biggest effect on our lives. Cars give people the freedom to go where they like, when they like – with some types of car you don't even need a road. Trucks are used for long-distance haulage and for performing many specialized tasks, such as fire-fighting. In parts of the world where there are no railways, trucks offer the only way of transporting goods. But cars and trucks create pollution. Because there are now so many of them on the roads, the world's cities have become clogged with traffic, and the air that many of us breathe is poisoned with traffic fumes.

A Benz Motor Wagen of 1886

Early cars

Early cars were called "horseless carriages". They were made by manufacturers of horse-drawn carriages and coaches, and had the same large wheels, high driver's seat, and suspension. They were powered by a single-cylinder petrol engine, which could reach a top speed of 15 kmh (9 mph).

Modern cars

Efficiency, safety, and comfort are the most important features of a modern car, as well as minimal air pollution from exhaust fumes. To be efficient, cars need engines that use as little fuel as possible, and a streamlined shape to reduce air resistance. In some cars electronics help efficiency and safety. Modern cars are built with the help of computers and robots in high-tech, automated car plants.

Henry Ford

American engineer Henry Ford (1863–1947) formed the Ford Motor Company in 1903. In 1908, Ford launched the Model T. It was made cheaply on a factory assembly line and sold by the million.

Stiff bodyshell is made from thin sheets of steel pressed into shape and welded together. It is chemically treated and painted to protect against rusting.

Windscreen of toughened glass protects driver and passengers from wind and rain. If hit by a stone, the windscreen cracks but does not shatter.

Side windows can be lowered.

Padded seats

Engine burns fuel and uses the energy stored within the fuel to propel the car along.

Bonnet is raised to examine engine.

Radiator circulates water around the engine to cool it.

Luggage is stored in boot.

Rear bumper

Exhaust pipe carries waste gases away from the engine and expels them at the rear of the car.

Hub-cap covers the centre of the wheel.

Suspension spring allows the wheel to move up and down as the car travels over bumps in the road, protecting passengers against uncomfortable jolting.

Driveshaft (or prop shaft) connects the gearbox to the rear wheels, which are driven round by the engine.

Gearbox contains intermeshing gear wheels that change the amount of power going to a car's wheels.

Pneumatic (air-filled) tyres grip the road and help give a smooth ride.

Front bumper

Luggage is carried in the boot.
Family saloon

Aerodynamic design enhances speed performance.
Sports car

People carrier/MPV
Three rows of detachable seats

Formula 1 racer
Wing
Driver's cockpit

Types of cars

The most popular car is the saloon, which has an enclosed passenger compartment and a separate rear space for luggage. Hatchbacks are saloons with a large rear door and a folding back seat for extra luggage space.

Sports cars

Sports cars are designed to be stylish, fast, and fun. Some sports cars are convertibles, which have a flexible roof that can be folded down so that passengers can enjoy driving in the open air. Luxury convertibles have roofs that open and close automatically.

People carrier

One of the latest types of car is the people carrier, or multi-purpose vehicle (MPV). This vehicle is a cross between a saloon car and a minibus. People carriers are very versatile, with at least six seats and plenty of space for luggage. They are perfect for outings or holidays.

Racing car

Some cars are purpose-built for racing. They have a very powerful engine, wide tyres, and a low, wide body for stability around fast corners. An aerodynamic "wing" on the back helps keep the car on the road at high speeds. Saloons can be converted into racing or rallying cars.

Trucks

Trucks are used for carrying cargo along roads. Their journeys can range from a few kilometres on local deliveries to thousands of kilometres across continents. The first trucks were built in the 1890s, and were driven by steam engines. Since then, trucks have grown ever larger. In Australia, trucks called road trains tow hundreds of tonnes of cargo across long distances in several full-sized trailers. Some trucks are "rigid", that is, built in one piece. Articulated lorries are built in two sections: a tractor unit and a semi-trailer, which is designed to carry specialized loads. Great skill is required to drive an articulated lorry.

Modern trucks

At the heart of most modern trucks is a powerful diesel engine, using diesel oil, a type of petroleum. Some diesel engines are turbocharged for extra power. The engine powers the truck, and operates any hydraulic parts, such as the lifting arms of a dumper. Some trucks, such as military vehicles, have chunky tyres and strong suspensions, to enable them to travel off-road in rough terrain.

Some trucks have up to 20 forward and 10 reverse gears.

A tractor unit and semi-trailer

Inside a truck cab

Long-distance truck drivers spend many hours in the cabs of their trucks. Cabs are designed for comfort, and some of the controls, such as the steering and brakes, are power-assisted to make them easy to use. Many cabs have a small rear room, with a bunk, washing facilities, and television. To help prevent accidents, some countries have introduced tachometers to record how many hours the truck is on the road. It is illegal for the driver to go beyond a certain number of hours.

Heating controls (temperature selector and fan speed selector) keep cab at a comfortable temperature in hot or cold weather.

Cassette, radio, and CB (citizens' band) radio provide entertainment on the road. Drivers may use CB to warn each other of traffic jams.

Adjustable nozzles allow fresh air into the cab.

Warning indicators light up if anything goes wrong with the truck.

Gauges, such as the speedometer, show speed, engine temperature, and the amount of fuel left.

Large diameter steering wheel is easy to turn with power assistance. This is known as power steering.

Gear selector   *Clutch pedal controls gears.*   *Brake pedal*   *Accelerator pedal*

Karl Benz

In 1886, German engineer Karl Benz (1844–1929) patented his first car, using an internal combustion engine. The car had electric ignition, three wheels, differential gears, and was water-cooled. In 1926, his company merged with Daimler to become one of the leading car and truck producers in the world.

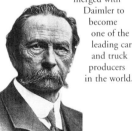

Research and development

Modern research aims at improving car economy, safety, and ecology. Because petroleum reserves are limited and its use is environmentally unsound, research is taking place into new fuels from sustainable sources, such as plant oils. Researchers are also experimenting with new materials for car parts, including plastics for car bodies. Car manufacturers are aware that making cars cleaner and safer is likely to improve sales.

Crash test dummy

Testing airbag inflation

Catalytic converter

Cars and trucks are gradually becoming "cleaner", which means they create less pollution. Most new cars have a catalytic converter, which removes carbon monoxide, nitrogen oxides, and other poisonous chemicals from the exhaust gases.

A catalytic converter from a car exhaust

Safety features

Manufacturers are constantly developing new safety features, such as airbags that inflate automatically in the event of an accident. They are also working on new ways of preventing accidents, such as anti-lock brakes.

Types of truck

Most trucks start life as a standard chassis and cab. Car manufacturers can then add the body, which determines the function of the truck. Common specialized trucks include rubbish trucks, flat trailers to transport large items, such as cars, tankers, fire engines, and vehicles modified to carry animals, such as horse boxes.

Rubbish truck

This truck has a closed container for rubbish and a rubbish-bin lift that empties a bin into the body through a protective shield.

Car transporter

A car transporter is used to convey cars to showrooms. There are ramps at the back which fold down at the rear so that the cars can be driven on and off. The trailer of a car transporter can carry up to 18 vehicles.

Storage space above the cab

Horse box

This truck carries horses to shows. The horse enters the truck via a door at the rear, which folds down to make a loading ramp.

FIND OUT MORE   BICYCLES AND MOTORCYCLES   ENGINES AND MOTORS   FORCE AND MOTION   OIL   POLLUTION   ROADS   TRANSPORT, HISTORY OF   TRAVEL   UNITED STATES, HISTORY OF

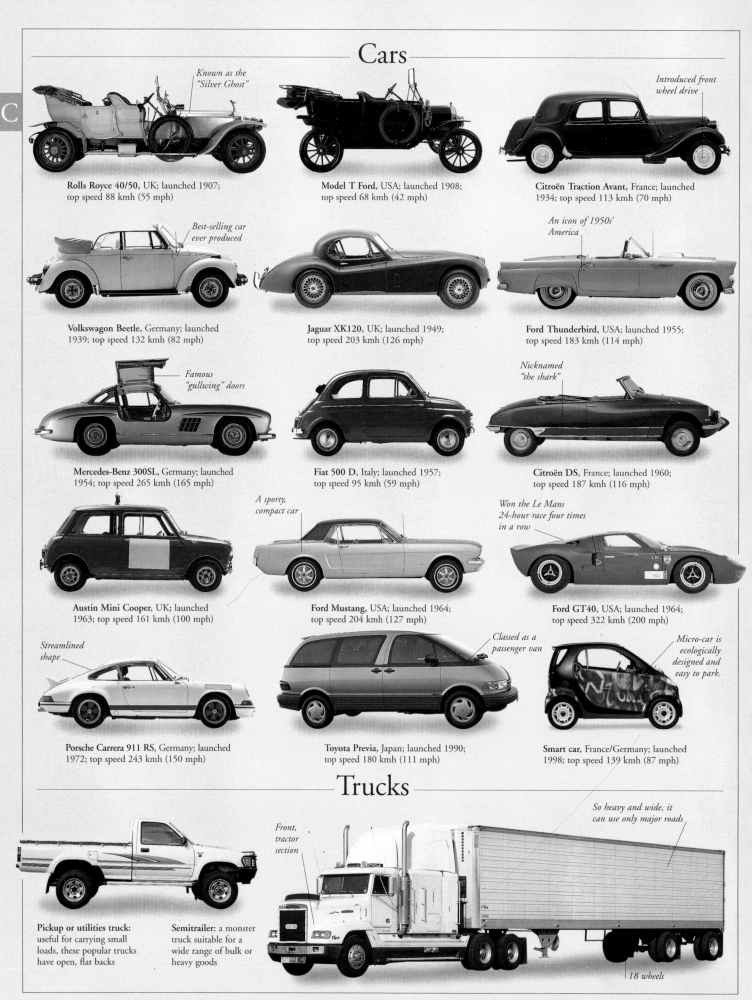

Cars

Rolls Royce 40/50, UK; launched 1907; top speed 88 kmh (55 mph)

Known as the "Silver Ghost"

Model T Ford, USA; launched 1908; top speed 68 kmh (42 mph)

Citroën Traction Avant, France; launched 1934; top speed 113 kmh (70 mph)

Introduced front wheel drive

Volkswagon Beetle, Germany; launched 1939; top speed 132 kmh (82 mph)

Best-selling car ever produced

Jaguar XK120, UK; launched 1949; top speed 203 kmh (126 mph)

Ford Thunderbird, USA; launched 1955; top speed 183 kmh (114 mph)

An icon of 1950s' America

Mercedes-Benz 300SL, Germany; launched 1954; top speed 265 kmh (165 mph)

Famous "gullwing" doors

Fiat 500 D, Italy; launched 1957; top speed 95 kmh (59 mph)

Citroën DS, France; launched 1960; top speed 187 kmh (116 mph)

Nicknamed "the shark"

Austin Mini Cooper, UK; launched 1963; top speed 161 kmh (100 mph)

A sporty, compact car

Ford Mustang, USA; launched 1964; top speed 204 kmh (127 mph)

Ford GT40, USA; launched 1964; top speed 322 kmh (200 mph)

Won the Le Mans 24-hour race four times in a row

Porsche Carrera 911 RS, Germany; launched 1972; top speed 243 kmh (150 mph)

Streamlined shape

Toyota Previa, Japan; launched 1990; top speed 180 kmh (111 mph)

Classed as a passenger van

Smart car, France/Germany; launched 1998; top speed 139 kmh (87 mph)

Micro-car is ecologically designed and easy to park.

Trucks

Pickup or utilities truck: useful for carrying small loads, these popular trucks have open, flat backs

Semitrailer: a monster truck suitable for a wide range of bulk or heavy goods

Front, tractor section

So heavy and wide, it can use only major roads

18 wheels

CARTOONS AND ANIMATION

CARTOONS, OR ANIMATED FILMS, are movies in which drawings or models seem to come to life. The effect is achieved by slight changes to the drawing or model between each frame of film. Animated films first appeared in the 1900s, and the art has developed alongside motion pictures; computer animation is now used to create amazing special effects in movies. Cartoons usually have a comic theme, although animation can also be a thought-provoking medium for a serious message.

Hanna-Barbera

The US animators Bill Hanna (1910–2001) and Joe Barbera (b.1911) created many of the most popular TV cartoon characters. Their first film, called *Puss Gets the Boot*, was released in 1940 and starred Tom and Jerry, the cat and mouse rivals. Other Hanna-Barbera characters include Yogi Bear and the Flintstones.

Tom and Jerry

Direct animation

With this method the animator creates characters from clay or other media. The characters are slightly repositioned before the camera between each frame of film, creating the effect of movement.

Clay model in an animated sequence

Step 1: figure starts out with his back to the camera.

Step 2: position is manually altered before next frame is shot.

Step 3: a sequence has been created which shows him turning around.

Scene from *A Close Shave* (1995)

Wallace & Gromit

Wallace & Gromit are the creations of British animator Nick Park and have starred in several award-winning films. The plasticine puppets are less than 15 cm (6 in) high. It took a budget of £1.3 million and a crew of 25 animators, modelmakers, and camera operators to make *A Close Shave*.

Key shapes

Traditionally, one of the most difficult areas of direct animation has been to show a character talking. Specific mouth and lip positions, called "key shapes", must be created for every word spoken. Today, computers can aid this process.

Cel animation

In cel animation, animators produce at least 12 drawings for each second of action. The background, which usually does not move, is drawn on paper. The animator draws the moving characters on layers of cel (clear plastic film), so there is no need to redraw the parts that do not move between frames. The background shows through the clear areas of cel.

Paints used to add colour

Background is drawn on paper.

Boy is drawn onto cel.

Clear cel strip

Chuck Jones

US animator Chuck Jones (1912–2002) drew the rabbit Bugs Bunny and many other famous characters in Warner Brothers' "Looney Tunes" cartoons. He directed his first animated film in 1938 and made 300 films in his lifetime, winning three Academy Awards.

Computer animation

Animators use computers to draw the images between the start and end of an action, or to improve or alter hand-drawn images. Computers can now generate an entire film, as in *Toy Story* (1996), as well as breathtaking special effects.

Aladdin

Aladdin (1992) was one of Disney's first major computer-animated films. Although the characters were hand-drawn, three-dimensional software was used to create dramatic effects in lighting, texture, and movement, such as the lava sequence.

© Disney

The Simpsons

Matt Groening created *The Simpsons* while still at school, publishing them as a newspaper comic strip. The animated series made its debut on US television in 1989 and has since become one of the world's most popular shows. The quirky storylines centre on Bart and his family.

The Simpson family

Homer

Marg

Maggie

Lisa

Bart

MATT GROENING

FIND OUT MORE   CAMERAS   DISNEY, WALT   FILMS AND FILM-MAKING   NEWSPAPERS AND MAGAZINES   PAINTING AND DRAWING

CASTLES

IN MEDIEVAL EUROPE, castles acted as both home and military stronghold. They were occupied by a lord, his family, servants, and sometimes an army of professional soldiers. They provided refuge for local people in times of war. Local lords could control the surrounding land from their castles, hence they were a very important part of feudalism. Castles were built to be defended, with walls strong enough to keep out an enemy, while allowing the occupants to shoot at any attackers. Designs changed as builders invented better methods of defence, or adapted new ideas from castles in the Islamic world.

The Chapel
Every castle had its own chapel. It was usually in an upper room in one of the towers. This is the chancel of the chapel at Conwy. The altar would have been beneath the windows, and there would have been enough room for everyone in the castle to gather together.

North-west Tower

Outer Ward

The Great Hall was the centre of activity. There was a high table for the lord and lady, and lower tables for everyone else.

The Kitchen was where food for the whole castle was prepared. There were wood fires, oak tables, and alcoves.

The Stockhouse Tower got its name when stocks for prisoners were made here in the 1500s.

The Inner Ward was the last refuge in time of attack.

Machicolations, or overhanging parapets, allowed defenders to pour boiling water on their opponents.

Chapel Tower

The King's Tower
This room on the first floor, close to the royal apartments has a stone fireplace and a recessed window. The recess means a person looking out remains safe from any enemy fire. The original floors have been removed.

The Prison Tower had a deep, dark dungeon.

Bakehouse Tower

King's Tower

Conwy Castle, Wales, in the 13th century

The East Barbican was the first line of defence against attack by sea, and was also a good position from which to fire. Defenders could isolate the enemy in this area.

Lookout Tower

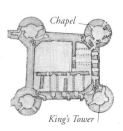

Chapel

King's Tower

Parts of a castle

Early castles had a keep, which contained the lord's rooms, hall, chapel, storerooms, and a well-defended gatehouse. Later castles abandoned the keep, and replaced it with a Great Hall, which was built against the castle walls. The lord's rooms were sometimes built into the gatehouse, but in Conwy they are in the Inner Ward, which was the heart of the castle, and most easily defended.

Timeline

1066 The Normans erect wooden motte-and-bailey castles during the conquest of England. These are quick to build, and the motte, or tower on top of a mound, is easy to defend. Most buildings are in the bailey, or courtyard.

Krak des Chevaliers, Syria

1142 Krak des Chevaliers built in Syria; one of the most easy-to-defend crusader castles, has concentric stone walls.

1127 Rochester Castle built: includes a great hall, chapel, and storerooms. The entrance is well protected, and defenders can shoot at attackers.

Great Tower, Rochester, England

1150 Many French lords build castles along the River Loire. Examples built (or extended) during this period include Loches, Chinon, and Montreuil-Bellay.

1200 The German lords of Liechtenstein build their castle on a high crag for extra defence.

Caerphilly, Wales

1238 The Muslim rulers of medieval Spain begin the castle-palace of the Alhambra.

1271 Concentric castles, like Caerphilly, become popular. They have rings of walls and sometimes water defences (moats).

How castles were built

Building a castle required many skilled workers. A master mason drew up plans and supervised the work, and less senior masons carried out the building. Carpenters did the woodwork, and metalworkers made hinges and door fasteners. In a large castle, some specialists stayed on permanently to do the maintenance work.

Wood and earthwork
The Normans chose a site where there was a water supply, built a mound and a wooden castle on top, and surrounded the structure with a wooden fence, or palisade. Most were replaced with stone constructions.

Motte-and-bailey

Stonework
Building a stone castle took decades, but the result was a strong castle that would withstand attack well. The important structures, such as the outer walls, mural towers, and keep, were all made of stone. Buildings in the castle courtyard were still made of timber and had thatched roofs.

Windows

Most castle windows were narrow or cross-shaped slits. They usually had a large alcove on the inside of the wall. This allowed an archer to stand to one side and avoid missiles while preparing to shoot.

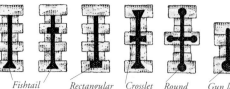

Fishtail bottoms   *Rectangular opening*   *Crosslet*   *Round ended cross*   *Gun loop*

Arrow slits developed that were large enough for a defender to shoot an arrow out, but too small for an attacker's missiles. Later, the gun loop developed with a circular hole to fit a gun barrel.

Edward I
In the early years of his reign, Edward I (r.1272–1307) conquered Wales, and built an "iron ring" of castles in strategic Welsh towns to keep the country under his control. Many of these Welsh castles, such as Harlech and Beaumaris, were built on the concentric plan, which meant they had both inner and outer walls for defence. Concentric castles were very difficult to attack successfully.

Asian and African castles

Castles have been built in many different places. There was a strong tradition of castle-building in the Islamic world, and medieval soldiers took Muslim ideas about fortification to western Europe when they returned from the crusades.

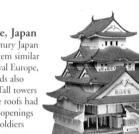

Himeji Castle, Japan
Seventeenth-century Japan had a feudal system similar to that of medieval Europe, and Japanese lords also lived in castles. Tall towers with pagoda-like roofs had narrow window openings through which soldiers could shoot. The towers were surrounded by courtyards and walls.

Fasilidas Castle, Ethiopia

The central stronghold shows many features in common with western castles, including thick walls of stone, round corner towers, and battlements. The remains of the outer curtain wall can be seen in the foreground to the right.

Van Castle, Turkey
Built on a rocky outcrop, Van Castle was begun in 750. It was later extended, and was occupied by the Seljuk and Ottoman Turks before being taken over by Armenian Christians.

Attack and defence

Attackers could fire arrows, hurl missiles using catapults, break down doors or walls with battering rams, climb the walls using ladders, or try to demolish the walls by tunnelling under them (mining). As well as defence features, such as thick walls and doors, moats, and machicolations, a castle also needed plenty of storage space for food so that the stronghold could withstand a long siege.

Arm

Rope to pull arm down again

Sling pouch

Wooden cup for missile

Ropes to winch arm down

Handle to turn ropes

Throwing arm

Hauling rope

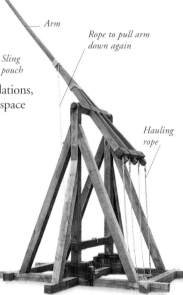

Crossbow
Crossbows were powerful but slow to reload. Despite this they could be useful in defending castles, where they could be reloaded behind the safety of the stone walls.

Catapult
The soldiers used a handle attached to a rope (made from a skein of twisted rope) to winch the throwing arm down. They then released it, and the arm flew up, releasing its missile, usually a rock, from a wooden cup.

Traction trebuchet
This siege engine was like a giant catapult. When soldiers pulled down on the ropes, the end of the arm flew upward, and the sling opened to release a missile, which usually weighed about 45–90 kg (100–200 lb).

Pfalzgrafenstein, Germany

Bodiam, England

1338 Many German castles are built on the Rhine because of the river's importance as a trade route.

1385 Bodiam Castle has a curtain wall around a courtyard, which contains the hall and chapel.

Real de Manzanares, Spain

1416 By this time many French castles, such as Saumur on the River Loire, have conical towers, strong defensive walls, and luxurious rooms.

1435 The elaborate Real de Manzanares is built.

1642 In Traquair, a Scottish tower-house, turrets and battlements are more for decoration than defence.

Traquair House, Scotland

1600s Many castles were built by local lords in Japan, like Himeji.

 FIND OUT MORE

ARCHITECTURE   EUROPE, HISTORY OF   FEUDALISM   MEDIEVAL EUROPE   NORMANS

CATS

DOMESTIC CATS are related to wild cats, such as lions and tigers, and they are able to fend well for themselves. They are excellent hunters, and their eyes, ears, nose, and whiskers are well adapted for their natural preference for hunting at night. Cats are affectionate and respond well to humans. They were domesticated about 4,000 years ago to keep people company and to destroy pests.

Kittens

Cats have an average of four or five kittens in a litter. Kittens love to stalk, chase, and pounce on things. This helps to make them strong, and develops the skills they will need as adults.

Domestic cats

There are more than 100 recognized breeds of domestic cat. They are distinguished mainly by their body shape. People started to breed cats for their looks between 100 and 150 years ago.

White | Lilac | Red | Blue | Chocolate

Siamese | British shorthair | Persian longhair | Devon Rex

Fur
Cats can be divided into long- and short-haired breeds. Fur is of various textures. Common coat colours are grey-blue, black, brown, white, red, and mixtures of these, such as silver and lilac.

Head shapes
Cat head shapes range from large and round, like that of the British shorthair, to wedge-shaped, like that of the Siamese. Some breeds have special characteristics, such as the Scottish fold, which has the tip of its ears bent forward.

Games enable kittens to practise hunting skills, such as stalking and catching.

Loose-fitting skin gives freedom of movement.

Flexible spine allows the cat to twist its body.

1 If a cat suddenly falls, balance organs in its ears tell it which way is up.

2 The cat turns its head around first so that it can see where it is falling, and where it is going to land.

3 Then the cat turns the rest of its body. By the time it reaches the ground, it will be the right way round.

Balance
A cat's long flexible tail helps it to balance. Cats will almost always land on their feet, even when falling from a great height. They have very quick reflexes and can twist and turn their body the right way up in a fraction of a second.

Back paws are brought forward.

Grooming
Cats are very clean animals and spend at least an hour a day grooming, using their tongue as a "comb". The tongue has tiny hard spines, called papillae, on its surface. The licking helps to keep the fur clean and waterproof, and also spreads the cat's scent all over its body.

Papillae

4 The cat stretches out its front legs to absorb the impact of landing.

Senses

Cats can see well in low light and can focus on small objects a long way away. Their super-sensitive hearing picks up sounds that we cannot hear and can also take in two sounds at once, such as a mouse in a thunderstorm. Whiskers are sensitive to touch. Cats use them to feel their way in the dark, and to measure whether spaces are wide enough for them to go through.

Ears are funnel-shaped to draw sounds inside the ear.

Long, flexible ears can turn toward sounds.

Cats rely more on eyesight than smell when hunting. They have the largest eyes in relation to their size of any animal.

Cats use their sense of smell to identify objects, other cats and animals, and food.

Sense of taste is important for distinguishing any food that may be harmful.

Claws
Cats use their claws to defend themselves and to climb. At other times, the claws are drawn in, or retracted, for protection. They are covered by a bony sheath that is an extension of the last bone of each toe and fit inside pockets in the skin.

Narrow pupils in the light

Large pupils in the dark

Changing pupils
A cat's pupils expand enormously in the dark to let in as much light as possible. A layer of cells at the back of the eyes, called the tapetum, reflects light back into the eye which helps cats see in the dark.

 FIND OUT MORE

ANIMAL BEHAVIOUR | EYES AND SEEING | LIONS AND OTHER WILD CATS | MAMMALS | MOUNTAIN WILDLIFE

Cats
Long-haired

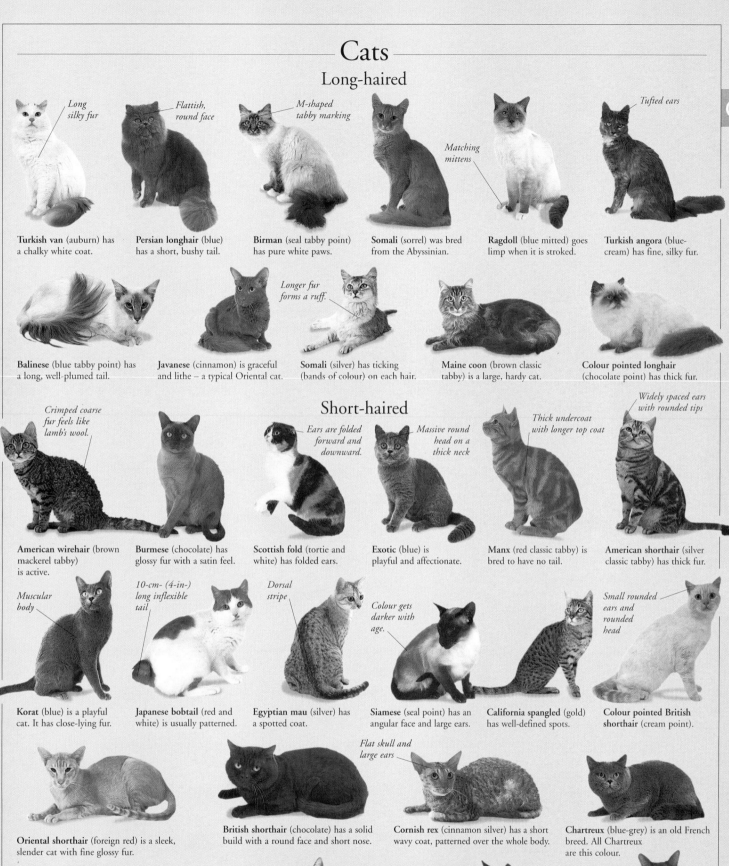

Long silky fur

Flattish, round face

M-shaped tabby marking

Matching mittens

Tufted ears

Turkish van (auburn) has a chalky white coat.

Persian longhair (blue) has a short, bushy tail.

Birman (seal tabby point) has pure white paws.

Somali (sorrel) was bred from the Abyssinian.

Ragdoll (blue mitted) goes limp when it is stroked.

Turkish angora (blue-cream) has fine, silky fur.

Longer fur forms a ruff.

Balinese (blue tabby point) has a long, well-plumed tail.

Javanese (cinnamon) is graceful and lithe – a typical Oriental cat.

Somali (silver) has ticking (bands of colour) on each hair.

Maine coon (brown classic tabby) is a large, hardy cat.

Colour pointed longhair (chocolate point) has thick fur.

Short-haired

Crimped coarse fur feels like lamb's wool.

Ears are folded forward and downward.

Massive round head on a thick neck

Thick undercoat with longer top coat

Widely spaced ears with rounded tips

American wirehair (brown mackerel tabby) is active.

Burmese (chocolate) has glossy fur with a satin feel.

Scottish fold (tortie and white) has folded ears.

Exotic (blue) is playful and affectionate.

Manx (red classic tabby) is bred to have no tail.

American shorthair (silver classic tabby) has thick fur.

Muscular body

10-cm- (4-in-) long inflexible tail

Dorsal stripe

Colour gets darker with age.

Small rounded ears and rounded head

Korat (blue) is a playful cat. It has close-lying fur.

Japanese bobtail (red and white) is usually patterned.

Egyptian mau (silver) has a spotted coat.

Siamese (seal point) has an angular face and large ears.

California spangled (gold) has well-defined spots.

Colour pointed British shorthair (cream point).

Flat skull and large ears

Oriental shorthair (foreign red) is a sleek, slender cat with fine glossy fur.

British shorthair (chocolate) has a solid build with a round face and short nose.

Cornish rex (cinnamon silver) has a short wavy coat, patterned over the whole body.

Chartreux (blue-grey) is an old French breed. All Chartreux are this colour.

Large pricked ears

Coat has a silvery sheen.

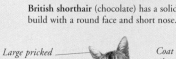

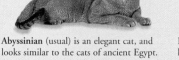

Tonkinese (cream) is a Burmese and Siamese cross. It is active and affectionate.

Abyssinian (usual) is an elegant cat, and looks similar to the cats of ancient Egypt.

Russian shorthair (blue) has a graceful, long body with thick, fine fur.

Oriental shorthair (Havana) was developed from a chocolate point Siamese.

CAUCASUS REPUBLICS

THE COUNTRIES of Georgia, Armenia, and Azerbaijan lie just within Asia, on a narrow plateau sandwiched between the Greater and Lesser Caucasus mountains. They are often collectively called Transcaucasia or the Caucasus Republics. To the west of the region lies the Black Sea, and to the east, the land-locked Caspian Sea. All three countries were part of the former Soviet Union and only gained their independence in 1991. Since the end of communist rule, growing ethnic and religious tensions have caused civil unrest throughout much of the region.

Physical features

Much of the land is mountainous and rugged, with large expanses of semi-desert in the Armenian uplands. The Kura is the longest river, flowing 1,364 km (848 miles) from central Georgia, through the fertile lowlands of Azerbaijan to the Caspian Sea. The low Black Sea coastal area in western Georgia is lush and green. The area suffers earthquakes.

Greater Caucasus Mountains

The Greater Caucasus range stretches for about 1,200 km (745 miles) from the Black Sea to the Caspian Sea, effectively separating Europe from Asia. Rich in copper, iron, and lead, the mountains also shelter the Caucasus Republics from the icy winds that blow down from Russia in the north. The highest mountain is Mount El'brus at 5,633 m (18,481 ft), just over the Russian border.

26°C (79°F)   0°C (32°F)

375 mm (15 in)

Regional climate
The varied landscape of this region gives rise to a wide range of climates. Georgia's Black Sea coast is warm and humid, while Armenia is generally dry with long, cold winters. The lowland areas of Azerbaijan have long, hot summers and cool winters. Winters in the mountains are bitterly cold.

Ararat Plains
Most of Armenia is a high plateau with large expanses of semi-desert. In the southwest, the land drops towards the River Aras, which forms the border with Turkey and drains most of Armenia. Known as the Ararat Plains, this fertile, sheltered strip is used for growing vegetables and vines.

Lake Sevan
Once valued for its pure waters and stunning setting, Armenia's Lake Sevan is at the centre of an ecological crisis. Tragically, irrigation and hydroelectric projects begun in the 1970s have caused the water level to drop by up to 16 m (52 ft).

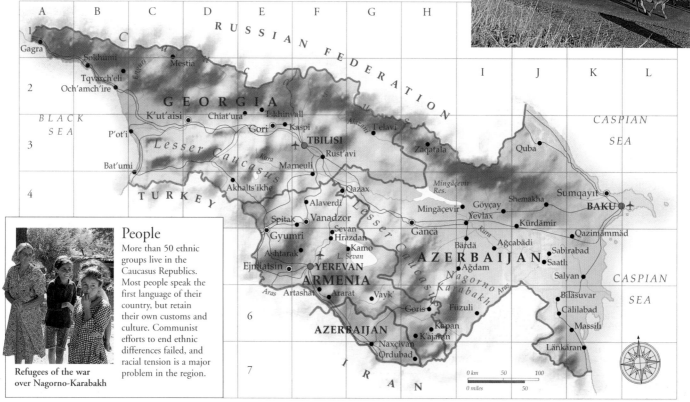

People
More than 50 ethnic groups live in the Caucasus Republics. Most people speak the first language of their country, but retain their own customs and culture. Communist efforts to end ethnic differences failed, and racial tension is a major problem in the region.

Refugees of the war over Nagorno-Karabakh

Georgia

Georgia is the westernmost of the three republics. About 70 per cent of the people are ethnic Georgians, most of whom belong to the Christian Georgian Orthodox Church. In recent years, the economy has suffered as a result of civil wars and ethnic disputes in the regions of Abkhazia and South Ossetia, which are trying to break away. This has damaged the Black Sea tourist industry.

Gold threads enhance bright patterns.

Textiles
Georgia produces fine silk cloth, and mulberry bushes, used to feed silkworms, grow well. Bright cotton fabrics are used to make the headscarves worn by so many of the Georgian women.

People
More Georgians claim to live for over 100 years than any other nationality in the world. Contributing factors are thought to be a healthy diet, regular exercise, a clean environment – and a genetic predisposition to longevity. Claims for ages over 120 have not so far been proved.

Tbilisi
Situated on the banks of the River Kura, Tbilisi, Georgia's capital since the 5th century, is a multicultural city of 1,200,000. Home to most of Georgia's Armenian minority, it has places of worship for many religions.

Tea and wine
More than 90 per cent of the tea sold in Russia is grown in Georgia, which produces about 250,000 tonnes each year. Georgia also has extensive vineyards and produces excellent red wines.

Armenia

Land-locked and isolated from its neighbours, Armenia is the smallest of the Caucasus Republics. The only way out of the country is by difficult road and rail links over the mountains to Georgia. The people, mostly ethnic Armenians, speak a unique language. The country exports fruit, brandy, and minerals such as copper.

Azerbaijan

The largest of the Caucasus Republics, Azerbaijan also has the most extensive area of farmland. Around 93 per cent of the population are Muslims. Most other people are Christian Armenians and Russians. Naxçivan, a separate part of Azerbaijan, lies within Armenian territory.

Cubes of meat are separated by peppers and onions for flavour.

Metal skewer allows cooking meat to be turned.

Oil industry
Natural gas and oil are extracted from the Caspian Sea. Pipelines link Baku, which is the centre of the industry, with Iran, Russia, Kazakhstan, and Turkmenistan. Other oil-related industries include the manufacture of chemicals and oil-drilling equipment.

Food
Lamb is the main meat, often served as kebabs, with a variety of vegetables. Cooks use pine-nuts and almonds for flavouring. Local cheeses and rich desserts are specialities.

Yerevan
Armenia's capital, Yerevan, is also its largest city. Situated on the River Razdan, it is a major cultural and industrial centre. Market traders sell fruit, vegetables, and rich, colourful rugs woven locally from silk and wool.

Territorial conflict
Nagorno-Karabakh, an enclave in southern Azerbaijan, has been the subject of armed conflict with Armenia since 1988. Most of the people here are Armenians, and Armenia claims the territory. A ceasefire was negotiated in 1994, but dispute over the area continues today.

Farming
Agriculture, mainly in the Aras river valley, employs 30 per cent of the work-force and is the country's main source of wealth. Crops include cereals and fruit such as apricots, grapes, olives, and peaches.

Soldiers on parade, Karabakh

People
Communal drinking of hot, sweet tea from tiny glasses is a typically male ceremony. As in neighbouring Georgia, the Azerbaijanis have a reputation for longevity, and it is not uncommon for people to continue working into their eighties.

FIND OUT MORE   ASIA, HISTORY OF   CHRISTIANITY   ENERGY   FARMING   ISLAM   MOUNTAINS AND VALLEYS   OIL   SOVIET UNION   TEXTILES AND WEAVING   TRADE AND INDUSTRY

CAVES

BENEATH THE GROUND, there is a network of large holes, or caves. Caves are naturally occurring chambers, formed out of rock. There are many different cave types, some housing hidden lakes and waterfalls; caverns are extensive networks of giant caves. Some caves are no bigger than a cupboard, but others are huge. The Sarawak Chamber in Malaysia is 700 m (2,296 ft) long and 50 m (164 ft) high; the world's biggest sports stadium, the Louisiana Superdome, could fit into it three times over. Damp and dark, caves have distinctive features, such as stalactites and stalagmites.

Types of cave

The biggest and most common cave systems are found in carbonate rocks, such as dolomite and limestone, but small caves form in all kinds of rock. Caves are found in many terrains, from the sea to glaciers, and can have different formations.

Sea cave
Small caves form in sea cliffs; waves force water into cracks, blasting the rock apart. The hole may emerge as a blowhole on the cliff-top.

Fissure cave
The movement and force of an earthquake can create deep fissures, long, narrow openings, and caves.

Ice cave
Greeny-blue tunnel caves form under glaciers after spring meltwater carves out passages under the ice.

Lava cave
Tunnel-like caves form in lava – surface layers harden, and molten lava flows underneath.

Limestone cave
Most caves form in limestone. This rock has many joints and its calcium content is vulnerable to the acid in rainwater.

How a cave forms

Most of the world's biggest caves are formed by water trickling down through soluble rocks, such as limestone. The water widens joints or cracks by dissolving the rock. Rainwater is dilute carbonic acid and wears away the rock, creating a cave.

Step-like rock formations

Stream emerges over waterfall.

Craggy limestone cliffs

Sinkhole – point at which a stream disappears.

Sparse vegetation

Ridges and grooves in the limestone surface are called clints and grykes.

Water seeps through rock joints; rock forms cracks that widen into potholes.

Icicle-like stalactites hang from the roof or walls.

Underground lake

Steep channel carved by stream.

Later passage eroded by stream.

Stalagmites grow up from cave floor.

Stream exits via cave mouth and flows along the valley bottom.

Groundwater fills a previously dry cavern to the level of the water table, which can rise and fall over time.

Cave features

Formed over thousands of years, stalactites and stalagmites are found in caves. Droplets of water partially evaporate to form calcium deposits (calcite); drips create hanging stalactites on the roof, and upright stalagmites where they fall to the floor. Spiralling drips form twisted helictites. Flowstone is solidified calcite on the cave floor or walls.

Stalagmite

Stalagmites and stalactites
Stalactites can form in different ways – a long, thin curtain stalactite is formed when water runs along the cave roof. When stalactites and stalagmites meet in the middle, they form a column. The biggest stalactite, 10 m (33 ft) long, is in Pruta do Janelão, Minas Gerais, Brazil; the biggest stalagmite is over 32 m (105 ft) tall in the Krasnohorska Cave in Slovakia.

Merged stalactites

Stalactite

Stalactite with ring marks

Curtain stalactite

Potholing

Potholes are the vertical pipes that lead down to many extensive cave networks. Today, potholing is a popular but dangerous sport. Exploring and discovering caves can unearth historic treasures. The caves at Lascaux, France, for instance, which contain a wealth of prehistoric wall paintings and tools, were discovered by potholers.

FIND OUT MORE   CAVE WILDLIFE   COASTS   EARTHQUAKES   FOSSILS   PREHISTORIC PEOPLE   ROCKS AND MINERALS   SPORT

C